VIRGINIA COLONIAL ABSTRACTS
SERIES 2, VOL.4
JAMES CITY COUNTY, VIRGINIA
1634–1904

COMPILED AND PUBLISHED
by
REV. LINDSAY O. DUVALL

This volume was reproduced from
A personal copy located in the
Publisher's private library

All rights reserved. No part of this publication may be reproduced,
stored in a retrieval system, transmitted in any form, posted
on to the web in any form or by any means without
the prior written permission of the publisher.

Please direct all correspondence and orders to:

www.southernhistoricalpress.com
or
**SOUTHERN HISTORICAL PRESS, Inc.
PO BOX 1267
Greenville, SC 29601
southernhistoricalpress@gmail.com**

Originally published: Easley, SC. 1979
Copyright 1979 by: Silas Emmett Lucas, Jr.
ISBN #0-89308-065-9
All rights Reserved.
Printed in the United States of America

JAMES CITY COUNTY.

THE SOURCE INDEX AND OTHER CONTENTS.

A. Sources
   1. Ambler Manuscript, from the Manuscript Division
      of the Library of Congress, Washington, D.C. .... 3 - 37
   2. Instructions, Etc., 1606-1633, one volume,
      Manuscript Division, Library of Congress,
      Washington, D. C. .... 37 - 39
   3. Foreign Business & Inquisitions, 1665-1675,
      one volume, Manuscript Division, Library of
      Congress, Washington, D. C. 39
   4. Land Patents, Books 6 & following, Archives
      Division, Virginia State Library, Richmond, Va. ...... 40 - 84

B. Additional
   1. Chart 2
   2. Source problems: (a) Date of the limits of
      Jamestown. (b) The office or Library from which
      the Ms. is copied of the Limits of Jamestown
      (James City County). 85
      The missing pages of Book. I of the Land Patents 85

ACKNOWLEDGMENTS.

I am indebted to the following Libraries for valuable services in the work that was necessary for this volume: (a) The Manuscript Division and the Rare Book Room of the Library of Congress; (b) The Archives Division of the Virginia State Library; (c) The Library of the Virginia Historical Society. Since the contents of this volume deal considerably with land records, I wish to express gratitude to Nell Marion Nugent for the advise and help which she has given me in the preparation of this work and in the general sense over a period of years. The original suggestion that a presentation of available records of James City County would be of value was made by the late Mary Pollard, formerly of the Archives Division of the Virginia State Library.

In preparing this work, the policy has been to include abstracts of all the contents of the Mss. volumes with specific James City County material. Thus, the dates are somewhat extensive, and material of other counties is included.

The index includes that of names and also that of places. An indexing large possibilities of grouping tended to form difficulties. Consequently, when the patents state the county is James City County or James City and other Counties, I indexed all places under James City County with cross references to the entry of the other county named.

CHARTS WITH NOTES.

JAMES CITY CORPORATION.
THE FOUR CORPORATIONS
1618 to 1634

Henrico	Charles City	James City	Elizabeth City

(when the counties were formed in 1634, these became counties from above)

Warwick River, later Warwick County.	Warrosquyoake, later Isle of Wight.	(M. P. Robinson, Virginia Counties, Bulletin of the Va. State Lib., Vol. 9, uses the following as authority. Alexander Brown, The First Republic, p. 313: "... James City and Warwick counties... and as the present Surry and Isle of Wight counties, or it may have extended to the Elizabeth River on the South side, as the South bounds are not definitely stated.	

JAMES CITY COUNTY,
formed 1634.

| James City County west of the Chickahominy was annexed to Charles City County, 1720, Wm. & Mary Quart., II, Vol. 18, p. 112. | Surry, formed 1652. | Exchange of the upper end of James City Co. for the lower end of New Kent Co. 1766, Hening, Vol. 8, p. 208. | Additions of Williamsburg (a) line of James City and York Counties, to run down main street in Williamsburg, 1769, from Hening, Vol. 8, p. 405. (b) the whole of Williamsburg, 1870 |

AMBLER MANUSCRIPT.

Ms. # 1.

The first item will be summarized, not abstracted. The subject is the legal background of English Law concerning patents. Citations are referred to, giving exact source references.

Ms. # 2.

John Harvey, Knight: Governor: Encouragement of building and peopleing of James Citty, It was enacted at a Grand Assembly holden ye 20:th of ffeb: 1636 .... grant unto Richard Kemp Esq. a parcel of Land, lying and being in James Citty, containing ten po: in length towards ye waterside, and eight po: in breadth, ye total being eighty po: between ye land of Mr. Thomas Hill and Richard Tree, etc. Dated ye 1st of Aug: 1638. Recorded Vo. 49: 1b 38. Copia Vera: Test Edw'd. Chilton Cl Off. Col. Edw. Chilton was Attorney General in 1697 (Note is in the Ms.)

Ms. # 3.

Att a Court holden at James Citty 13th: of 8ber: 1641. Present Sr. Francis Wyatt, Knt., Gov'r., Capt. John West, Mr. W:m. Brocas, Capt. W:m. Peirce, Mr. Amb: Harmer, Mr. Geo: Menefye, Mr. Rich'd. Bennett, Lease for 21 years to ye Rt. Wor'pel: S:r ffrancis Wyat Knt., Gov'r. for 50 Acres of Land in Pasbyhaies, as also yt. a Pattent be granted unto ye sd: Francis Wyatt Knt. for three acres of Land in James City Island, adjoining unto Mr. Rich'd. Kemp, and since conveyed unto ye sd Sir Francis Wyat by ye sd. Mr. Kemp
  Copia Vera.   Teste Edw'd Chilton Cl Off.

Ms. # 4.

Indenture, 23 March 1648, Between the Hon. Sir Wm. Berkeley and Walter Chiles of James Citty in Va. Gent. of ye other part ... sold ... miessuage ... lyeing & Being in James Citty, late in ye occupation of Rich'd. Kemp Esq. and by him conveyed unto Sir ffrancis Wyatt and purchased by ye (blank) sd. Wm. Berkeley of Capt. Wm. Ferrer, attorney of ye sd. S;r ffrancis Wyatt ... together with one pcell of ground granted to ye sd. S:r ffrancis by ord:r of Court conteyning three acres more or less and being in James Citty aforesaid adioning to ye land whereon ye sayd messuage standeth ... (The seal appears to be real.)

Ms. # 5.

Edward Diggs Esq. do give and grant unto John Bauldwin 15 Acres 69 po: James Island between the Main river &the back river bound (Vizt:) ten acres part thereof easterly upon Mr. James his land North upon the back river and the land hereafter mentioned west upon the main river and south upon the Slash which lyeth between the state house & ye sd Mr. James & five acres 6 po: the residue at the old block house beginning at the head of a marsh swamp Issueing into the back river but running to the blocke house belonging to the backe river southerly to a red oak on a point near the first mentioned land thence south 3/4 west 4 po: soe west 1/2 part north 36 po: to the place it began ... 4 Oct. 1656.
Copia   Test Ralph Gouge & C C Thacker Cl Soc Off.

Ms. # 6.

Indenture, 5 Aug. 1658, between Edward Hill of Charles Citty County Va Esq. and Elizabeth his wife, 1st part, & Walter Chiles of James Citty in Va. aforesaid Gent. of ye other part ... sold one Brick house Scituate in James Citty being ye next house on ye west road and of Mrs. Rix her house, and now in ye possession of ye said Edward Hill.

Wit.: Mathew Edloe &   Signed Edw: Hill &
     Edward Sanderson, Jr.   Eliza: Hillum her Mark
              James Citty, Aug. 6, 1658
              Acknowledged in Court Teste Ric. Esterwether Cl Ct.

Ms. # 7.

At a Quarter Court held at James Citty 17:8ber:1660. Present: Sr. Wm Berkeley Knt. Gov'r: Coll. Hen: Browne, Coll. Guy Molsworth, Coll. Rich: Lee, Coll. Thomas Dewe, Coll. Fran: Moryson, Coll. Obed: Robins, Coll. Wm. Bernard, Coll. Abra: Wood, Coll. Edw: Hill, Lt. Coll. Edw'd Carter, & Capt. Augustine Warner. Whereas Mr. Edmond Shipdam and Elizabeth his wife the late Relict of Rich: Reekes Dec'd. hath petitioned ye court in behalf of John Reekes orphant, sonn of ye sd. Rich'd Reekes Dec'd., for disposition and selling of a Brick house at James Citty, belonging to him as heir to his Father ... the house to be sold.
     Copia Vera   Test Edward Chilton sd. Com.

Ms. # 8.

Bk at a Grand Assembly held at James Citty in Va., 23 March 1661, whereas 11°B Elizabeth Chidman alias Perkins hath appeared by her agent Maj. pa: 52 Theophilus Hone before this assembly, 27 Acres, scituate in the Order 3. Main near James City, & by Jurie, o Apl.1661 ... escheated - no heires of ye said Thomas Parkins was existent (as in the Ms.) ... granted to Hon:able ffrancis Morrison, 16 May 1661.

Ms. # 9.

For the building and peopleing of James Citty Island ... by Grand Assembly, 2 March 1642, ... Grant unto Mr. William May half an Acre of Land in James Citty, bounded Southerly with the Land reputed (to be that of) Mr. Chiles Westerly and Northerly with the Land of John Phipp, and Easterly with Wast Land, running Easterly and Westerly eight po: and Southerly and Northerly 10 po: In as large and ample manner to all interests and purposes as is expressed in a charter Company dated 19 Nov. 1618 & ... Given at James Citty, 20 May 1661.

Ms. # 10.

John Knowles of James Citty paid John Phipps of James Citty ... sell ... the said John Knowles the Brick house commonly called and known by the name of ye County house ... lying in ye precincts of James Citty which said house and Land formerly belonged unto ye County ... unto Major Richard Webster and (by him) assigned unto Richard Rix dec'd and by Elizabeth Shydman on ye behalf of ye heyr of ye said Richard Rix Dec'd. according to an order of ye Hon. Gov. & Council, 17 Oct. 1660 sold ... unto the said John Phipps ... 5 Oct. 1661.
Wit.: Hen. Randolph   The Mark of
      Tho. Brereton   John Hooper
(Note: The signature is as given above) On the back of the Ms.: John ffyps acknowledged this in court, 4 Dec. 1661. Mary his wife, examined, acknowledged it, 4 Dec. 1661. John Knowles acknowledged it, 23 April 1667. John Knowles do acknowledge to have given possession unto Jonathon Newell of the within specified saile, 18 April 1668.

Ms. # 11.

Nathaniell Baconn Esq. and Elizabeth his wife ye daughter & heyr of Richard Kingsmill dec'd was paid by Nicholas Meriwether, 30 April last past, and assigned to Nicholas Meriwether Land Scituated in James Citty Island commonly called the Island house Bounding as followeth Westwardly By or Without an old Ditch Cross ye old ffeild nigh ye great popler Northwardly by ye Marsh or Back Creek Eastwardly By Back Creek and Kingsmill Creek Southwardly by ye Marsh or Kingsmill Creek and by a Branch of Pitch & Tarr Swampe. The said Land beinge formerly in ye possession of Richard Kingsmill dec'd. as is due unto ye sd. Elizabeth Bacon as being ye daughter & hey of ye sd. Rich'd. Kingsmill, 25 Nov. 166_.

Wit.: Rodger Porteridge   The Mark E B of Elizabeth Bacon
       John Bush   Signed by Nathaniel Bacon

Ms. 12.

Grant of Land is given to Nicholas Meriwether, 80 Acres, James City Island, Bounded Viz. Southerly on Kingsmill Creek and Easterly on the Main River and Northerly on ye back Creek and Westerly on a small Creek on Mr. James his land and thence to ye place it began. The said Land being formerly planted and seated by Richard Kingsmill deceased who was an Ancient Planter in this County and by Nathaniel Bacon Esq. and Elizabeth his wife the onely daughter and heyr of ye said Richard Kingsmill assigned unto ye said Nicholas Meriwether for the transportation to two persons whose names are in ye records, 26 Nov. 1661
(The names not given.)   Signed Francis Morryson.

Ms. # 13.

Grand Assembly, James Citty, 2 Dec. 1662, According to Order of Quarter Court, 17 Oct. 1660, impowering Edmond Shipdam & Elizabeth his wife late Relict of Rich'd. Reeks Dec'd. to dispose of and sell a Brick house at James Citty for the use and behalfe of Richard Reeks Orphan Sonne of the said Reeks Dec'd. be by this Assembly ratified & confirmed
                                 Teste Robert Beverley
Whereas Edm'd Shipdam & Elizabeth his wife the late Relict of Rich'd. Reeks Dec'd hath petitioned this Court on behalfe of Rich'd. Reeks orphant, sonn of the said Reeks dec'd. for the saile.

Ms. # 14.

At a Court held in Henrico County, 14 Feb. 1664, Present: The Hon. Coll. Thomas Steggs Esq., Mr. Wm. Baugh, Lieut. Coll. Tho. Kegan, Major Wm. ffarrer, Capt. Francis Epes: Commissioners. Whereas Mr. John Knowles of this County but formerly of James Citty sould unto Mr. Johathon Newell of the County of York Merchant land therunto belonging in James Citty. The deed is dated 23 April (and in margin:) 1667. Whereas Botheia the wife of the sd. John Knowles hath Dower in the said Brick house lands and other tenements, she gives consent. Her consent in writing follows in the Ms.

Ms. # 15.

Land Grant is given to John Knowles, James City County, "pt within & pt without ye libertys of the sd. Citty," 133 Acres, 35 cha & 9 Dec., Beginning at a Corner Stakt by a ditch neere ye house formerly belonging to John Phipps thence along ye said ditch ... 7 neere a branch of pitch & tarr swamp ... to a marked red oake neere a small marsh ... including a small point formerly in difference, but found to belong to John Phipps ... upon a point against Mr. Nich: Meriwethers sleered ground ... on ye South side of a Cart pa the to ye Island house ... on ye North side of pitch & tarr swamp about 3 cha: above a bridge thence over ye sd: branch West by South 11 cha: to a corner stake att ye corner end of Mr. Walter Chiles's ditch, thence ... from ye Southwest and of Mr. Knowles his now swelling howse, thence ... to a corner stake neere ye Southwest corner of his old Garden, thence to a corner stake att ye other corner next to Mr. Wm. May his house, thence ... to a corner stake att ye corner of ye garden next the howse formerly (of) John Phipps, thence ... The said Land being due to ye said John Knowles as followeth: 120 Acres purchased of John Phipps as by a conveyance dated ye 13 day of 10ber 1663 & recorded in ye records of James County Court: 3 Acres, 44 cha: 37 Dec: pts. due to ye said John Knowles by purchase from John Pjipps who purchased from ye relict of John Rix on land apperteyning to a brick howse now in James Citty but ye sd. Knowles doubting Phipps's sayle made an humble recon to ye hon.:ble Governor & Council who imediately confirmed yt sale as by an order of yt Court bearing date 17 of 8ber 1660 may more fully appre which said order was confirmed by an order of Assembly as by ye

5

Records may more fully apre. The Remainder of ye said land being 9 Acres: 71 cha: 53 Dec: pts. being due unto him ye sd. John Knowles by & for ye transportation of one pson unto this Colony whose name is on ye record mencoed under this pattent, 6 May 1665. (No name is given.)

Ms. # 16.

Land Grant to John Knowles, James City Co., part within and part without ye said citty containing 133 Acres: 35 cha: 9 Dec: pts. Beginning (the same description is given as above), 12 Sept. 1662 & 6 May 1665.
Teste: Phill: Ludwell Cl Off.   Signed William Berkeley.
On the other side: I John Knowles of Henrico County ... sell ... the within written pattent ... deed of sale, 23 April 1667, James Citty Co.
Wit.: Hen. Randolph   Signed & sealed John Knowles
    John Elwood & Tho. Gardner.

Ms. # 17.

Richard ye son of Richard James and Rachel his wife was born the 14th day of Decem:r 1660 about 5 in the afternoon. Copy of ye Register. Teste Chris: Smith Cl Psh. May ye 6th 1704.

Ms. # 18.

Land Patent to William May, 100 Acres of Marish Land, James Citty Island below Goose Hill bounded (Vizt:) Northerly on the land formerly (of) Major Holt now in the possession of John Barber northerly on John Pinhornes, North East on Parchmores Creek, South East on the Maine River, South West and South East on Will Sarsuett & South West on the Maine River. The said Land being formerly unto Thomas Woodhouse and by Will Hookere by pattent, 21 July 1657, and by them deserted and upon petition of the said William May It was granted unto him by order of ye Gov'r. and Councell bearing date with these presents, due for the transportation of two psons, whose names are on the records, 15 April 1667.
(Names not given.)   Teste Tho. Ludwell.   Signed William Berkeley.

Ms. # 19.

Bill of Jonathon Newell to John Knowles, 150 li. Sterl. & 20,000 li. of good Tobacco, etc., 23 April 1667. Wit.: Hen. Randolph, John Elwood and Tho. Gardner.

Ms. 20.

John Knowles of Henrico County to Jonathon Newell of York County, acknowledging the payment of above, 23 April 1667. Condition: Deed of Sale to Jonathon Newell, Land in James Citty. The same wit. as above. 28 April 1668. Deed with seal. Recorded by Rich Awborne Ct Con.

Ms. # 21.

Land Grant to Richard Holder, 8 Acres, 1 Rd., & 5 Perches, in James Citty, bounded as foll. Vizt. Beging at a stake standing at high water marke on James River side at ye mouth of a small rum entering thereunto thence running No: Ea: ... neere to ye corner of the Orchard So: Ea: ... to a stake on ye Bank near James River Side thence No: W: ... along ye River side to ye place where it began, 28 Jan. 1672.
    Copied.   Test Hen: Hartwell Cl Off.
    (In later hand:) All in the Autograph of Henry Hartwell.

Ms. # 22.

Land Grant to Richard Holder, same acreage and description as above the said land being granted unto him the said Richard Holder by an order of the Gen:ll Court held at James Citty, 12 Oct 1670 and due unto him for the transportation of one person, 20 Jan. 1672. (The name is not given.)

Ms. # 23.

To the Hon:ble (the Ms. is worn, so part of the word is blank)
   embly of Virg:a:
The Inhab:ts & greeholders of James Citty Humbly p:sent.
   That ye sd. Citty according to Capt Smiths discovery of Virg:a was dated in ye yeare _607 (worn) & hath ever since beene ye seate of ye cheife Courts or Judicature & Metropolis of this his M:ies (Colony is crossed out) Country & dominion yett ye certain

M:d	limitts & bounds, hat not by any publiq A(c)t or Instrument
this	beene ascertained, although by report of ye Ancient Inhab:ts
Act	itt begins at ye Sandy Bay & so included all ye (crossed out:
was	Land between River & Creek from thence to ye run or slash by
drawn	Wm. Briscoe ye Smith & soe to ye gack creek) Island (Margin:
up &	All ye Island) We humbly pray yt ye said bounds be ascertained
passed	by Act of Assembly and whereas by one act of ye last Sessions,
ye	of Ass:bly itt was enioyned yt 50 Acres of land should be
howse	laid out for a town in James Citty at ye rate of 1000 li. tob:
Apll	co. We humbly inform Yo:r hon:es yt ye land in the sd. Citty
1682.	is of considerable value & not an acre there by cost about 5

li. Sterl: besides our great charg in building.
And therefore wee humbly ppoase, yt ye & ye owners of the Land in ye sd. Citty may have lib:ty to build Store howses there (in case itt be enioyned P & if we fayle, that then any others may have land assigned y:m by ye County Co:rt upon paym:t of so much as ye land shall be valued att, by an able Jury, according to ye Law & presidents of Engl:d in ye like cases: And yt ye Whole Island may be assigned to build on.
And for yt itt is our desyre yt all nusances & corrupones of ye Air may be hereafter removed: & ye City for ye future kept clean & decent w:ch can not well be done without a law (worn) se, & ye pticular ways & means to effect ye same (worn) tedious & troublesome to direct & set down, we humbly pray yt as Lib:ty is given to ye severall countys of this Colony to make by Laws: soe authority may be given to ye sd. Citty to make such By Laws as shall be a greed (as in the Ms.) on by ye freeholders & howsekeep:s for ye better governing & conveniency of ye sd. Citty & inhabitants thereof. And Whereas there is a Marsh in James Citty Island not hitherto taken up or pattented by any which by order of the Rt. hon:ble ye Governor & Councill, was & is to lye in comon for all ye gen:ll hab:ts of James Citty, we humbly pray that the said order of ye gen:ll Court may be confirmed by Act of Assembly.
Copies at James Citty 1682   Signed Wm. Sherwood
                                      Tho. Parson
1 - 16 - 0   Wm. Homins
   10
2 - 6 - 0

(Note: The above is a copy. There are several problems to be considered. The Manuscripts have been mounted by someone in chronological order. The manuscript is not dated. It seems logical to suppose that the person who mounted the manuscripts considered its date as that of 1673, since the items before and after this item are of the year 1672/3 and 1673.
   This item has been printed twice: (a) Va. Mag. of Hist. & Biog., Vol. 12, p. 199, with the date of 1682; (b) Cradle of the Republic, by L. G. Tylor, and he argues for the date of 1682. A Third point is that these printings omitted the statement given above that the item was copied in 1682.
   A second problem is concerned with the interpretation of the signatures. Thus: (a) Va. Mag.: Tho. Sherwood, Tho. Parsons, Wm. Edwards; (b) Tyler: Wm. Sherwood, Tho. Claton, Wm. Harrison; (c) as above given. The last two signatures are almost impossible to read

with certainity. There is a necessity for further scholarship. - L. O. D.)

Ms. # 24.

Indenture, 20 Nov. 1673, Between James Wadding of the parish and County of James Citty Clerke, and Susanna his wife, late the wife, & Executrix, of Walter Chiles of James City aforesaid Gent. dec'd., of the one part & John Page of the Parish of Brewton in the County of York Merchant, of the other Whereas by indenture bearing date 23 March 1649, Between the Rt. Hon:ble S;r William Berkeley ... of the one part, & Walter Chiles of James Citty aforesd. Dec'd. (ffather of the aforesaid Walter Chiles) of the other part ... sell ... messuage ... in James Citty, then late in the tenure & occupation of Richard Kempe Esq. and by him conveyed to S:r ffrancis Wyatt Knt: and pruchased by the said Sr. William Berkeley: of Capt. William Poires, Attorney of sd. ffrancis Wyatt, together with one pcell or plott of ground, granted to the sd. ffrancis Wyatt, by order of Court, conteyning & by estimation three Acres ... in James Citty aforesaid Walter Chiles the father dyed (Leaving the said Walter Chiles (late husband to the said Susanna W adding pty to these prsts) his eldest son & heir att law) ... said Walter Chiles the Sonn being seized of a good estate in fee simple ... 15 Nov. 1671, he the said Walter Chiles the Son, made his last will and testament in writing, and Susanna his then wife (now Susanna Wadding pty to these presents) Sole Executrix thereof, and in the said will, amongst other things therein conteyned, did direct & appoint that his brick howse ... in James Citty should be sold, and the produce thereof to be added to the said Walter Chiles Estate: Shortly after the makeing of which will the said Walter Chiles the Son dyed... Now this Indenture witnesses that the said James Wadding and Susanna his wife ... mansion howse, heretofore in the possession of the said Richard Kempe Esq. and late in the possession of Thomas Tully, And also ... Messuage ... built by the said Walter Chiles the Son, lately in tenure & occupation of Maj. Theophilus Hone, ...
 Signed with
 two seals.   Jam: Wadding, Sr.
        Susanna Wadding.

Ms. # 25.

Nicholas Meriwether Executor of the last will & testament of William May dec'd ... received of Major William White of James Citty County ... sold ... two halfe acres of land, Jas. City, being the land whereon the said William May Lived, Bounded as by Pattent and order of ye Genn:all Court ... 6 Feb. 1677.
Wit.: Hen: Hartwell
  Richard Clarke Signed with Signed Ni: Meriwether.
        seale.
  6 Feb. 1677/8, Acknowledged in Court.
    Hen: Hartwell Cl Cur.

Ms. # 26.

David Newell, the only Brother & he-ir of Jonathon Newell, late of York County Merchant Dec'd ... David Newell did by Deed, 7 Feb., 1675, assign ... to Coll. Wm. Claiborne Jun:r & Wm. Sherwood A Certain Messuage ... belonging formerly in ye possession of Major Theophilus hone which he holds as tennant to my said dec'd Brother, ... land ... in James Citty. To be held to them ye sd. Col. Wm. Claiborne & Wm. Sherwood ... as by ye said Deed Recorded in James Citty County Court Appeareth, and whereas said Wm. Claiborne & Wm. Sherwood, by two deeds, dated Last of October Now last past ... assigned ... to me ye sd. David Newell ... only except to the said Sherwood & his heirs, the said howse ... and one Acre of land lyeing next & adioyning to ye sd. howse ...
Wit.: James A Aesupp
  his mark   Recorded 23 April 1678
  Richard James Test Hen Hartwell.

Ms. # 27.

Indenture, 21 May 1679, Between Thomas Hollday of James City, of one part, & William Briscoe of James Citty, of the other part, Whereas John Barber and Lettice his wife by their deed of Assignment, 7 Dec. 1664, unto James Alsopp ... the one halfe of the halfe Acre of Land neare adjoyning to the howse of the said John Barber, in James Citty, which the said Barber formerly purchased of Mr. William Drummond ... Thomas Holliday as executor of James Alsopp ... sell ... unto William Briscoe.
Wit.: Edw. Harrison   Signed Thomas Holliday
     William W Tisdell his marke   Probably a seal once attached
               Rec. 6 Jan. 1679 Jas. Citty.
Acknowledged in Court by Thomas Holliday above and Hana his wife,
        & is Recorded. Test Hen Hartwell

Ms. # 28.

Whereas att a Gen:ll Court held att James Citty, 12 Nov. 1679, Martin Gardner, Attorney of Stephen Proctor of London, recovered a judgm:t for moytie of ye Lands of Jonathon Newell Dec'd of a Deed of 269 li. ... Due by ye said Newell to ye said Proctor ... Wm. Cole Esq. Attorney of Spencer Piggott of London, did recover ye likewise judgem:t for an Extent Act one moyetie of ye said Newells Land to satisfy a debt of 214 li. shewd due by ye said Newell to ye sd. Piggott, As thereby appeared, And for yt ye reall estate of ye sd. Jonathon & w:ch are Extendable by ye said Judgm:t and as followeth (Vizt.) A plantation or tract of land in York old fields on which ye sd. Jonathon lived, conteyning about 500 Acres, Another pcell of Land on w:ch a Mill formerly stood, formerly belonging to George Gill, ... York (CO.), Another pcell of Land scituate at James Citty of w:ch remained 132 Acres, 35 cha: & 9 Dec. pts., And ye right to a pt. of ye Mill & land att Skiffs Creek in possession of David More, which are all ye Lands yt can be Extended toward paym:t of ye several debts aforesaid ... Wm. Cole Esq. Attorney of ye said Spencer Piggot accepts ye Land before mencon in York County, ... and ye sd. Martin Gardner Attorney of ye said Stephen Proctor shall accept of ye Land in James Citty with ye right to ye Mill att Martin Hundred and a debt due by Ambrose Slane ... 16 April 1680.
Wit.: Robert Spring   Acknowledged in Court 16 April 1680
     Wm. Sherwood.   & Recorded. Test Henry Hartwell Cl Con.

Ms. # 29.

Inquisition, James Citty, in James Citty County, 12 July 1680, before Edward Sanderson Sheriff of ye County aforesd., Inquisition annexed, by the oaths of (names are given, the same as listed at the end) who say upon their oaths yt David Newell in ye writ aforesd. named ye 25 Nov. 1679 at ye time of ye granting of ye judgment in ye aforesd. writt specified was seised of 132 Acres, 15 cha: & 8 Dec. pts. of Land in ye Right of & descent to ye sd. David Newell as Brother & heir to Jonathon Newell in ye writ & judgment mentioned, in his demesor as of fee (?) with its appurtenants lying & being in James City in ye County aforesd., as by an assignment of a Patent from John Knowles to Jonathon Newell ... 23 April 1667 ... by a survey ... 6 Aug. 1664 and by ye hand of John Underhill Surveyor ... one moety of ye sd. Land being 66 Acres, 7 cha: & 9 Dec. pts. to be of ye clear yearly value of 66 shillings ... besides reprisals to ye sd. Martin Gardner in ye sd. writ mentioned as Attorney of Stephen Proctor ... until full satisfaction of ye debt ... 269 li. 10 s ... signed (all signatures with wax seals attached) Edward Sanderson Sheriff, Thomas Clayton, Henry HT Thompson, Geo: Marable, Sen., Thomas Bobby, Thomas T Radley, his mark, Richard Winter, his mark, Alexander Walker, Ben: Egleston, Robt. Ashers, John Deane, Jabe E Belomy, his mark, & Tho: Milton. Sept. 1680, Rec. in ye off. Test Hen: Hartwell Cl Con.

Ms. # 30.

19 Aug. 1680, before Willm. Scorey notary & tesbellion Publicke ..

appeared Winnifred Proctor of London aforesaid Widdow the relict and
Executrix of the last will & Testament of Stephen Proctor late of
London aforesaid Merchant deceased, P/A to Martin Gardner of York
River in Virg. ... Martin Gardners former endeavors by virtue of the
P/A of the said Stephen Proctor against the estate of Jonathon Newell
dec'd. ... satisfaction ... of all debts ...
Wit.: Thomas Brookhouse   Sealed and delivered by Winnefred Proctor
      Philip Hawthorne   Wit.: Robt. Conaway & Zack:y Taylor.
(In another hand-writing) Sworne to in Court by Robt. Connawaye Capt
         Zachary Taylor, 24 Feb. 1680 & Rd Cl Cur Ebor.
         Recorded (in Latin) Guil. Scorey.

Ms. # 31.

Land Patent to William Sherwood, 28½ acres, at mouth of James
Citty Island and is bounded as followeth (Vizt.) beginning at James
River at the head of a great slash Issuing into the bask River and down
the Slash East ... to the back River Marsh and up the same to a markt
persimon tree under blockhouse hill point thence under the said hin
west 5 cha: to James River and down it again to the first mentioned
Slash including 8 Acres & thence down the Said Slash 43 cha: to Mr.
Richard James Land and along it South 23 cha: to a branch of Pitch &
Tarr Swamp thence up the said branch to James River and up the River
to the place it began conteyning 20¼ Acres of the said Land being
formerly granted to John Baldwin by pattent, 24 Oct. 1656 for 15
acres, 59 perches more or less and now by a late Survey found to
conteyn 28½ Acres. And the said John Baldwin by his last Will &
Testament in writing under his hand and seal did give the said Land to
John ffulcher and his heirs for ever which said John ffulcher by Deed,
22 Oct. 1677 acknowledged & recorded in James Citty Courty Court
sould and conveyed the same to the said William Sherwood, 23 April
1681.
   Copia Teste Thhacker Cl C C Thacker Cler Off.

Ms. # 32.

Land grant to Mr. William Sherwood one Acre, James City, on which
formerly stood the brick house formerly called the County house which
said howse _____ belonged to the County and by the Hono:ble
Assembly was sold and assigned to Major Richard Webster and by the
said Webster assigned to Richard Ricks dec'd and afterwards by an
order of the Hono:ble Governor & Councell, 17 Oct. 1660, was sold to
John Phipps who amongst other lands sold and conveyed the same by deed
under his hand and seale, 5 Oct. 1661 ... to John Knowles ... John
Knowles by deed, 23 April 1667, ... conveyed ... amongst other lands
to Jonathon Newell ... who dying w:thout issue the same descended and
came to David Newell brother and heir at Law ... And the said David
by deed of sale ... 6 Feb. 1677 ... sold ... to the said William
Sherwood... Mr. William Sherwood hath since new built a faire howse ...
which said acre of Land beginnes at a stake before Coll. Whites cove
then running towards his howse etc. ... to the place it begun ...
23 April 1681. Signed Hen. Chicheley.
Compared & agrees with the Record. Test Nicho: Spencer Secr:ty.
(Notes in the text. A square paper added in the left corner, probably
a faded plan, with ref: see Knowles Plan. See Tyler, p. 53.)

Ms. # 33.

Indenture, 6 Feb. 1681/2, Between Martin Gardner of York County
Gent.Attorney of Winnefrid Proctor of London Widdow Execu:r of the
last will & testament of Stephen Proctor late of London Merchant dec'd.
of ye one pt., and William Sherwood of James Citty Gent. of ye other
pt., whereas Jonathon Newell late of York County Merchant did heretofore purchase of John Knowles, 133 Acres, 5 cha: 9 Dec: pts. of land
... James Citty ... John Knowles ... 18 April 1668 ... which said
Jonathon Newell dyed ... descended to David Newell brother & heir at
law to the said Jonathon ... the aforesaid Land (excepting one acre
on w:ch the brick howse stood & w:ch was before sold by ye said David
to the aforesd. William Sherwood was by order of the Gen:ll Court,

25 Nov. 1679) extended to sattisfie a debt of 269 li. 7 s. Sterl. due by judgm:t to the said Jonathon Newell and a debt of 214 li. Sterl. due by ye said Jonathon to Spencer Piggott of London by Judgm:t ... William Cole Esq. Attorney of ye said Spencer Piggott did sell ... to the said Martin Gardner Attorney of ye said Spencer Proctor ... said Stephen Proctor by his last will & testament in writing made the said Winifreid Executrix thereby devising ye right of ye said Land to her Assigns, & ye said Winnigrid by writing or P/A, 19 Aug. 1680, proved & Recorded in Yorke County, to Martin Gardner to sell ... the said Martin ... all & singular the estate ...
Wit.: John Page   Signed & sealed   Martin Gardner
      Jno: Steward. 6 Feb. 1681/2 Ack. in Court.
      Test: Edw: Harrison Dep. Cl.

Ms. # 34.

Surveyed, 27 Oct. 1682, for Mr. Wm. Sherwood, 3½ Acres, James Citty Island bounded as followeth beginning at S. W. corner of his Acre of Land & coming N. ... to Pitch & Tatt Swamp & down it ... to his form:r Land and along ye same ... to ye place it began: Including ye Runn of Kemps old Brick house ...   Signed Jno. Soane.
Other side: Certificate of ye Survey of Land bought of Coll. Page.

Ms. # 35.

Land Grant to William Briscoe, 12 Acres, in James Citty and County, which William Penn died seized of and found to Escheate ... Coll. John Page Escheator of the said County and a Jury ... 24 May 1683 ... granted unto the said William Briscoe ... 20 Sept. 1683.
              Signed: Nichol: Spencer.

Ms. # 36.

(Left corner is torn away.) Sheriff to impannell a Jury to make Inquiry into what Land and tenements Coll. William White late of ye sd. County (of James Citty) dyed seized of & whether he left any heir, to be returned to the Secretary's office the end of May ...
29 May 1686.   Signed E Hingham.
          Approved by John Page Escheator.

Ms. # 37.

Inquisition, Jas. City County Court, 20 Sept. 168_, John Page Escheater, by commission, 30 April 1686, & by writ, 29 May last for an Inquisition ... William White, late of this County, died ... The Jury ... Lands before Mr. William May late of James City, was Seized of half an Acre of Land in James City, by Patent dated, 20 May 1661, And of half an Acre of Land Adjoining thereunto to him by order of the Gen:l Court, 21 June 1670 ... 1671 did give all his Land in James City to one Nichoas Meriwether and his heirs for over ... Nicholas Meriwether by deed, 6 Feb. 1677 ... did sell to Lt. Coll. William White, Land Nicholas Meriwether was bequeathed by the last will of William May, 7 March 1671, the said two half acre of Land which he died in possession of ... William White made no disposition of the said Land by will or otherwise, nor is there any heir of the Said White in this County to our knowledge ... Verdict ... Escheated ... (All the signatures are with wax seals:) John Page Escheator, Tho: Milton, Will: Briscoe, Rich: Hodge, James Hubbard, John Wilkins, William She___ (worn), M Sacke(?), Robt. Ashers, Ben: Egleston, George Lee, Thomas Holliday.

Ms. # 38.

The Nuncupative Will of John Holder dec'd. John Holder upon his decease ... I give to Mr. Wm. Briscoe a Mare & colt & all the tobacco he owes me towards ye discharge of "sunerall" charges, and all the rest of my Estate both Reall and personall. I give and Bequeath to my Loving Sister Anne Holder ... Except one Cow Calf I give to John Hall with its female Increase ... 8 Aug. 1687.

Att a County Court held at James Citty 8 Aug. 1687
The above will was proved by the oaths of John White (signature) and Dorothy Peach (her marke). Test W Edwards Cl Cur, Rec. 11 Aug. 1687.

Ms. # 39.

Whereas John Holder late of this Colony dec'd. Disposed of his Estate by a Nuncupative Will, In care whereof Anne Holder Sister to ye sd. dec'd. hath made humble suit to ye Court that a Commission of Administration might be granted unto her ... according to an order of James Citty County Court, 8 Aug. 1687. Administration is granted to her.
(blank space) Oct. 1687. E Hingham.

Ms. # 40.

Land Grant to henry hartwell, 2 Acres, one Rood, 24½ Po: James Citty, bounded as followeth, Beginning at a Stake, faced on ye Bank of ye River and thence by a Line Passing along by ye Angular Points of ye Trench w:ch faceth two of ye Eastern Battions of an old ruined(?) Turf ffort North ... Eastward ... where it butts on a Line of ye Lands now or Late of Mr. Sherwood, thence ... East South East, Thence ... North North East ... thence East ... thence East South East and South South West ... and East ... and South ... where it butts on ye Land now or Late of Holder thence along Holders South South West ... and thence by ye Lands now or Late of Thomas Rably along ye Northern side of an old ditch ... along by ye Western Side of ye same Land Late of Rably ... thence along ye Lands Late of James Alsop ... thence along ye Bank side of ye River up West ... to ye stake where it began, half an Acre of ye sd. Land by Patent, 20 May 1661, was granted to Mr. William May who by his will bequeathed ye same to Mr. Nicho. Meriwether and ye sd. Mr. Nicho. Meriwether by his deed of Sale, 16 Feb. 1677 ... sell ... to Mr. W. White, who dying without heirs of said Land ... Escheated ... an Inquisition ... granted ye sd. Mr. Henry Hartwell ... and one other half Acre ... by ye sd. Hen: Hartwell purchased of Coll. Jno. Custis, 29 Sept. 1683 ... and ye remaining being Wast Land found adjoyning ... granted to ye sd. Hen: Hartwell by order of Gen:ll Court, 28 Oct. 1688. ... transportation of one pson... 20 April 1689. (No name is given.) Signed Nathaniel Bacon.

Ms. # 41.

I Martin James of Wapping, Co. Midds (England) Ropemaker, a release and quit claim ... unto William Sherwood of Va. now resident in London ... 20 March 1690.
Wit: W Dall, belonging to ye Navy office   Signed   Martin James.
    Pattience e Allen.   & sealed.

Ms. # 42.

Indenture, 28 April 1690, between Edmond Jennings of the County of York in Va. Esq. and Wm. Randolph of the County of Henrico in Va. ... Land ... in the County of Henrico, 6,513 Acres ... sold ... unto the said Wm. Randolph ... the full one half of the said tract or divident of land containing by estimation 3,256 Acres being the lower part of the said divident ... beginning upon the uppermost line of Westham att a great red oak upon horsepen run and running West ... North ... for the breadth, and from thence down to the Creek of the Island South ... West ... to a great Ash by the Creek side for a corner tree and from the said Ash to the back line along a line of Marked trees North ... East ... and thence down the said line of the patent ... to the place begun at ...
Wit.: I Sedwick   Signed   E Jenings
      Stapleton Mank.   ffrances Jenings

At a General Court held at James City 29 April 1690. Edmond Jenings Acknowledged the Sale in Court. Teste Wm. Edwards C.G.C.

Also Wm. Sherwood for ffrances Jenings relinquished her right of dower, 20 May 1690. A copy of teste made by John Brown C. G. C.

Ms. # 43.

Land Grant to William Sherwood Gent., 150 Acres, James Citty Island, formerly granted to Richard James by patent, 5 June 1657 and descended to Richard James his Sonn ... Escheat ... C. Wormley Escheator of ye said County ... Jury ... 25 April 1689 ... granted unto Wm. Sherwood ... 23 October 1690.   ffra. Nicholson.
Recorded William Cole Sen.

Ms. # 44.

10:10ber:1690 for Henry Jenkins, 76 Acres, in ye Maine, bounded from James River on ye lowermost part of the Swamp whereon he lives & ye lowermost Ditch of his Plantation to Green Spring Road & down it towards Town to New bridge & along it to Mr. Geo: Loe:s & along it ... to a Gumm ... thence along Mr. William Drummonds lines ... on the upper part of ye first mentioned Swamp & cross the same to ye next lower branch thereof & along it or ye Gutter or valley thereof to James River & down it to ye place it began. Thirty five Acres thereof (between ye Road & ye River) being formerly in ye tenure of Ro. Lide & 41 Acres ye Residue.   Jn. Soane.

Ms. # 45.

Survey & Platt of Henry Jenkins Lands of 76 Acres, Surv:d 12 Dec. 1690. The Platt is given in these manuscripts.

Ms. # 46.

At a Gen:ll Court held at James City the 31st Day of October in the fifth year of their Maj:s Reign Annoj Dom:o 1693

His Esq. Sr. Edm:d Andros Knt. Gover:r etc., Ralph Wormeley, Esq., Sec. Edw:d Hill Esq., Richard Lee Esq., Hen: Whiteing Esq., Ch:r Wormeley Esq., Hon: Hartwell Esq.

William Sherwood Gent. compained against Thomas Welbourne --- debt --- 107 li. Sterl. --- Gener:ll Court, Jas. City, 28 April 1690, the said pet (with Thomas Arnold Since Dec'd.) obtained judgment against sd. def:t for Present payment of 60 li. Sterl. with interest and cost, And whereas also the said def:t by a certain bond ... 15 Oct. 1685 ... bound with one Dan:l Jenifer Gent. Since dec'd. to the said Thomas Arnold and the said pl:t in the penal sum of 40 li. Sterl. ... due 20 April 1690 ... not yet paid the said sum of 60 li. Sterl. ... And the def:t came into Court and confess Judgment to the pl:t for 80 li. Sterl. with interest ... and the interest of the said 20 li. due by the condition of the said recited bond from ye 20 April 1690. Judgment is granted for the same 80 li. Sterl. to the said Sherwood with interest.
Copia Test   R. Beverley Cl. Sec. Off.

To arrest Thomas Welbourne ... until he shall have fully satisfied and paid this Judgment unto the said William Sherwood. To the Sheriff or his deputy with   Signed   R Beverley
listings of debt.   Cl Sec Off.

Ms. # 47.

William Sherwood of James City Gent. ... to my Loving Nephew John Jarrett have given ... Land, 28½ Acres, James City Beginning on James River at the head of a great Slash issueing into the back River and down the sd. Slash ... to the back River Marsh and up Same to a marked persimon tree under blockhouse hill Poynt Thence under the sd. Hill West 6 cha: to James River and down it to the first mentioned Slash including 8 Acres and thence again down the sd. Slash 43 cha: to a Branch of Pitch and Tarr Swamp Thence up the sd. Branch to James

River and up the River to the place it began with ... purchased of John ffulcher and was afterwards granted and confirmed to me by Patent dated 23 April 1681 ... except allwaies reserved out of this guift and Grant 2 Acres of Land or thereabouts by me the sd. Wm. Sherwood heretofoe Leased to one John Hopkins and for 3 Acres now in possession of one ffrancis Bullivant and the fee simple and Inheritance of the sd. 2 Acres ... Appoint my Loving ffriends Capt. Michael Sherman and Mr. Poynes Weldon my attorneys ... 30 Dec. 1693.

Wit.: George Marables
    Peter Heyman
    Robert Beverley

Signed Wm. Sherwood
Court, Jas. City Co., 7 April 1694
Vera Copia C C Thacker Cl Cur.

Ms. # 48.

William Sherwood of James City Gent.
   (Gift and description as above.) Copia Test Jos. Davenport

Ms. # 49.

This Indenture, 6 Jan. 1693/4 Between William Sherwood of James Citty Gent., of one pt., & ffrancis Bullivant of the same place of the other pt ... Demise grant, and to farme lett to ye sd. ffrancis Bullivant, 2 Acres, James City County, bounded Westerly by James River Southerly by the Slash or Branch yt pts this Land & the State house, Easterly by the great Road, & Northerly by ye sd. Slash that pts. this land and the block house Land ... except ½ Acre of Land for a Landing & a Store if the sd. Wm. Sherwood or his assignes shall have Occasion for ye same.

Wit.: P Perry
    Edward Ross

Signed & sealed

ffra. Bullivant

Ms. # 50.

Land Grant to John Howard, 172 perches, James Citty, bounded from the North East Corner of the Church yard along the railes thereof ... to the Hon;ble Nathaniel Bacon ... to the Great road & along the same to the first mentioned Corner the said Land being due unto the said John Howard ... transportation of one pson. ... 20 April 1694. (No name is given.)

R Wormeley Sec: E Andros

Ms. # 51.

Land Grant to Robert Beverley, 3 Acres, one Rood & t po: James City, bounded as followeth beginning at the Southerly End of the Ditch which divides this from the Western side of the Lands late of Lawrence, Coll. Bacon or one of them at the road side Extending Northward along the Ditch ... to a slash called Pitch & Tare Slash or Swamp, then along up that Slash till it come to the Maine Cart road Westward makeing good in a right line 33 po: then down that cart road South Eastwards as it windeth but making good a right line 61 po: to the place it begun, the Said Land ... Importation of one pson (the person is not names), 26 Oct. 1694.

R Wormeley Sec.   Signed E Andros

Ms. # 52.

Gent.   London, 14 Nov. 1694

Mr. Wm. Sherwood haveing this day made composition with us for all arreares of quitt rents due to Michall mass last past for a tract of land called Doegs Island, 4400 acres, in Potomac River in the Northern Neck of Va. ... accept of a new grant from us... grant to be passed of ye said Island called Doegs Island to the said Wm. Sherwood ... under annual rent of one shilling for every 50 Acres ...

To Coll. Wm. ffitzhugh
  && Capt. George Brent
Our agents for the Northern Neck of Va.

Signed Marguerite Culpeper
    Fairfax
  Catherine Fairfax
  Alexander Culpeper

Ms. # 53.

Patent to Willm. Sherwood for 308 Acres, James City Island, 1694 Do to Henry Hartwell for 2½ Acres, Jas. Town, 1689 sold to William Edwards by Deed, April 1695 & by Edwards to Willm. Broadnax by deed 1709.

Patent to Jno. Howard for 172 Perches, land in Jas. City, 1694, beginning at N. E. corner of Church yard & running N. 87 Deg. Westerly 3 cha: & 90/1000 to N. Bacons Land along it N. six cha: x 8/10 to the corner thereof thence South 85½ Deg. Easterly 1½ cha: to a great old Road along of same to ye first mentioned Corner.

Bauldwins Patent for 15 x 69 perches in James City Island 1656 by him given John ffulcher & by him conveyed to W. Sherwood who had it surveyed & took out a new patent viz.

Patent to W. Sherwood for 28½ Acres at ye Mouth of I C Island which he gave by deed to his nephew John Jarrett 1693 reserv of 2 Acres & he sold to John Howard 1699 & by him sold to John Baird 1710 together with ye ½ Acre granted to ye said John Howard by Patent described before. Both these Parcels viz. ye ½ Acre near ye church & ye 28½ Acres at Block House Hill sold by Bair to Travis 1717 to Broadnax 1719.

Patent to Robert Beverley for 3 Acres & 1 Reed & t pole, Jas. City, 1694 & by him sold to William Broadnax 1718 for 110 li. Sterl.

Patent to Edw'd Ross for 5 Reed & 7 pole at ye head of Pitch & Tar Swamp in Jas. City.

Pat. to W. May for 100 A. Marish in J. C. 1667 called Goose Hill.

Patent to Briscoe for 12 Acres in J. C. 1683.

Chudleighs Deed to Edwards of 127 pole in J. I. 16796/7 by him assigned to W Broadnax 1709.

Baird Deed to Travis for the half Acre near the Church & 28½ Acres at Block House Hill 1717 & sold by Travis to Broadnax in 1719.

37 A. granted by Pat. to Coll. Sisan & by Coll. Sisan assigned to Rich'd. Holder together by will of said Holder to his Sister Ann Holder together with 8 Acres which were patented by sd. Holder in J.C. Ann Holder married Briscoe, his father by will gave her all his Lands in J. C. & heirs forever one parcel cont'g a quarter of an Acre in which Town Briscoe bought of Thomas Holiday ye Ex:tor of James Alsopp, who bought ye same of John Barber.

Bullivant to Broadnax of 107 A. 1736

Ms. # 54.

Land Grant to William Randolph Esq., 1221 Acres, Henrico County and in the parish of Verina & on the North side of James River & above Westham Creek Vizt. beginning at the Mouth of Westham Creek & the Mouth of a branch of Tuckahoe Creek & runeth thence by the branch of Tuckahoe Creek as it Tendeth to Tuckahoe Main Creek thence crossing that Creek West by South 8 poles being the breadth of the Creeke thence up Tuckahoe Maine Creek as Tendeth to a corner Elm thence 60 po: to a Corner Ash thence North 7 po: to a Corner black oake thence West North West 260 po: to a corner pine thence South South West po: to a corner black oake thence South West 34 po: to a corner black oake on James River thence down the River as it Tendeth to the place it began, The said Land was formerly granted to Mr. John Pleasents by Patent, 20 Oct. 1692 and by him deserted and since granted to the said William Randolph Esq. by Order of the General Court, 23 Oct. 1694 ... Importation of 25 persons (names not given), 21 April, 1695
Signed E Andros

V.º 7   A copy Test Wm. Claiborne
p. 408.   for Ben Waller.

Ms. # 55.

Deed of Indenture, Henry Hartwell of James City Esq. ... paid by William Edwards of Surry Co., Gent. ... sold unto said William Edwards, 2 Acres, one Reed, 24½ pole, James City, granted to me by Pattent, 20 April 1689 ... Rec. 23 April 1695.
Wit.: James Blair   Signed with   Hen: Hartwell
      ffra. Meriwether   seal
   Jane wife to the above named Henry Hartwell, Relinquishes Right of Dower, 23 April 1695.
Same Witnesses.   Signed with seal.   Jane Hartwell.
   At a General Court, Jas. City, 23 April 1695: Acknowledgement of Henry Hartwell of the deed & of Jane his wife, relinquishing her Dower Rights. Test R. Beverley Cl. Gen. Cur.

Ms. # 56.

Articles of Agreement, made 1 June 1695, Whereas ffra. Meriwether of the one part & Wm. Sherwood of the other ... ffra Meriwether ... sell ... to Wm. Sherwood a plantation know by ye name of the Island House ... in James Citty Island now in possession of Thomas Decket, 80 Acres by Patent ... with ye rent due as October next from Tho. Decket.
Wit.: Wm. Roscow   Signed: Thomas Deckit
      Willy Wilson   seal probably lost.   Francis Meriwether

Ms. # 57.

10 July 1695 for Mr. James Chudleigh & Ann his wife a pcell of Land in James Citty, 65 po: bounded from a stake on James River bank North ... of ye N. W. End of Rably brick house 11 68/100 po: to a Stake in Mr. Edwards line & along it North ... to a Stake on ye River bank & down it South ... to ye first stake. The sd. Land Viz. one quarter Acre thereof belonging to ye said Ann by ye last will of William Briscoe Dec'd. who purchased it of Tho: Holliday by Deed dated 21 May 1679 and with Surplass of 25 po: more being due sd. Chudleigh & Ann his wife ... Importation of 1 pson (person not named). Surveyed by Jn. Soane.

Ms. # 58.

Francis Meriwether, of Essex Co., Gent. ... indebted unto Mr. Wm. Sherwood ... 100 li., 21 Oct. 1695.
   Condition: Sale by ffra Meriwether to ye sd. Sherwood, 80 Acres, in Jas. City Island. Francis Meriwether.
Wit.: John Jane(?). Signed & probably once sealed.

Ms. # 59.

Indenture, 11 May 1696, between William Sherwood of James City, Gent., on ye i pt. & John Harriss of ye same place on ye other pt. ... sold ... unto ye sd. John Harris ... Land ... in James City aforesd., being part of a arcell of Land purchased by ye sd. Sherwood of John Page Esq. late dec'd. being late in ye occupation of Mr. Secretary Wormeley bounded as followeth (Vizt.) beginning at a Stake in ye Line on Omoonees Land formerly Hitcheiks Land & running along on ye South side of ye Mulberry trees 90 foot thence No:ly towards ye maine road forty foot, thence N. W. near ye sd. Maine Road to ye Corner of Omoonees Land 100 foot & so along ye line of Omoonees Land to ye place or stake it first began.
Wit.: Dionisius Wright   Signed with   John Harris.
      John Watson   seal.

Ms. # 60.

ffra. Meriwether of Essex Co., bound to William Sherwood of Jas.

16

City Co., for 100 li. Sterl.
   Condition: Wm. Sherwood did in Oct. last draw bills of exchange
... lost ... hath now received new bills ...
Wit.: R. Spicer &   Signed and
      Antho. Dowtin.   probably sealed.   Francis Meriwether
Below, several bills are listed   10 Sept. 1696.

Ms. # 61.

   Land Grant to Lievt. Edward Ross, James Citty whereon he now
dwells, 5 reed and 7 pole. Bounded from a Stake in the Corner of an
old Ditch Near the head of Pitch & Tarr Swamp, partly along the said
Ditch North ... to James River Banck and sown it South ... to a Stake
thence South ... (line mostly too worn to read) North (?) deg:
Easterly 6 44/100 parts to the first stake. One half an Acre of the
said Land was formerly granted unto John Phipps by Patent, 4 May
1661, and by him deserted and since granted unto the said Lievt. Ross
by order of the Hon:ble Generall Court, 15 April 1698 and a patent
being newly taken up and is due unto the said Lt. Edward Ross ...
Importation of 1 pson ... 29 Oct. 1696.
On this Ms. is: 1734   Signed E Andros
                  1696
                  ————
                    38

Ms. # 62.

   George Marable of the pish of James Citty Gent. son and heir
of George Marable late of the said pish dec'd. ... sold ... William
Sherwood ... Land ... James Citty, ½ Acre, on which a brick house
formerly stood and wherein my said father George Marable lived
abutting on and Joyneing Easterly to the brick howse and land now in
possession of John Everett belonging to Micajah Peary and Company
Merchants in London on the ruins of the brick Howse & half Acre of
Land belonging to Philip Ludwell Esq. Southerly on James River &
Northerly towards the howse & lands belonging to John Harris Taylor ...
12 Nov. 1696.
Wit.: James Omoonees   Signed &   Geo: Marable.
      John Harris   probably sealed.
   Memorand;M that I Mary, the wife of ... George Marable ...
relinquishment of right of dower & P/A to Mr. Dionisius Wright to
Acknowledge relinquishment.
Wit.: Ralph Bee   Signed &   Mary Marable.
                        once sealed.

Ms. # 63.

   James Chudleigh and Ann my wife Daughter of Rich'd Holder dec'd
to William Edwards ... pcell of Land in James City, 127 poles, from a
stake on James River banke along the Land late of Thomas Rably dec'd.
North ... to the said Edwards Land, and along it South ... to the Land
the said Chudleigh lives on late belonging to Richard Holder dec'd.
by Patent dated 28 Jan. 1672, and along the said Land South ... to a
stake at the Mouth of the Orchard Runn on James River and thence
North 42 deg. Westerly up the River 9 po: to the first stake ... unto
the said William Edwards
.... 5 Feb. 1696/7
Wit.: Wm. Sherwood.   Signed & sealed   James Chudleigh
                                           Ann Chudleigh.
   (On the back:) I Wm. Edwards of Surry Co., Gent., doe assign ...
unto Wm. Brodnax of James Citty ... 6 April 1709, Wm. Edwards.
   Court, Jas. City Co., 6 April 1709.
      Recorded Test Na Robertson.

Ms. # 64.

   Land Patent to William Sherwood, James Citty Gent., 308 Acres
in James Citty Island att the head of a branch of Pitch and Tarr
Swamp nigh about the statt howse and runing alson the North side
thereof to a ditch dividing the Land of the said William Sherwood and

the land formerly belonging unto one Thomas Woodhowse thence along the said ditch South 10 deg: Westerly over the said ditch & branch of pitch & tarr Swamp, to the 3½ Acres of land, which the said William Sherwood purchased of John Page Esq. and along the same the said Course in all 23 cha: to a mulberry three neere the land of John ffitchett, thence South ... to the Acre of land the said William Sherwood purchased of David Newell, brother of and heir att law of Jonathon Newell dec'd., and along it South ... towards the dwelling howse of henry hartwell Esq. thence North... thence along one Acre ... the said William Sherwood purchased of the said David Newell ... to the uppermose corner of the orchard belonging to James Chudleigh and Ann his wife and along the back thereof, over a branch of pitch and tarr swamp, to the lower corner of the said orchard, thence East ... South ... Easterly ... South ... Easterly ... North ... Easterly 20 Cha: to a gum on pitch and tarr swamp, South ... to a widd oak in Mr. Travis' line and along itt North ... to a pine on the South side of pitch side of pitch and tarr Swamp and down the said Swamp to a dead oake on pyney point, thence over the said Swamp or pitch and tarr marsh, North ... to a gum in a sharp point of land, thenceover another marsh North ... to a point of Swamp and along the North side of the swamp thereof to a lone of markt trees, and along itt North ... to a corner oak of the land, formerly belonging to Richard James, and along itt North ... to back River Marsh, and the same course 40 cha: through the Marsh to the River and up the same to Sandy bay to a persimon tree on the block howse hill thence under the said hill West to James River, and sown itt to the head of the first mentioned branch, The said 308 Acres being due and belonging to the said William Sherwood as followeth, that is to say, 3½ Acres, purchased by him ... of John Page Esq. as appeared by deed ... 6 Feb. 1681; 133 Acres, & 35 cha: & 9 Dec. (other part of the 308 acres) being heretofore granted by pattent, 6 May 1675, to John Knowles who conveyed the same to Jonathon Newell ... 28 April 1668 and since purchased by the said William Sherwood of David Newell; 28½ Acres (other part of 308 Acres) formerly granted by patent dated 4 Oct. 1656 to one John Baldwin, who by his last will and testament did give the same to John ffulcher ... and the said John ffulcher by deed 22 Oct 1677 ... conveyed the same to the said William Sherwood ... The Remainder of the said 308 Acres of land, being formerly granted to Richard James by a pattent, 6 Jun. 1657 and being lately found to Escheate was granted to the said William Sherwood by pattent, 23 Oct. 1690...
Rec. 20 April 1694   R Wormeley Sec.   E Andros.

Ms. # 65.

In the Name of God Amen I Wm. Sherwood of James City ... I desire that my body may be decently buried at the East end of the Church at James City without the Walls and I desire that my good friend Jeffrey Jeffreys of London Esq. to send a grave stone to be Laid upon my grave with this Inscription here Lies William Sherwood of White Chappell near London a great Sinner Waiting for a Joyfill Resurrection. It. I give to such poor of the parrish of White Chappel as Jeffrey Jeffreys Esq. Mich: Perry Merchant Mathew Bateman and Joseph Beyforth of the parrish aforesaid or any two of them shall think fitt ten pounds Sterl. It. I give to the poor of James City Parish ten pounds Sterl. to be Disposed of by my Loving wife Rachell and my good friend Wm. Edwards and Capt. George Marable or any two of them. It. I give to Eliz. the Daughter of John Jarrett fifty pds. Sterl. to be deposited in the hands of Mr. Micajah Perry of London Merchant till the said Eliz. attain the age of 16 years or be married but if the said Elizabeth shall Die before she attain the aforesaid age or marriage then I give the aforesaid fifty pounds Sterl. to Johannah the wife of John Jarrett to be paid her or any other person by and under her hand. It., I give to the children of William Myer and Eliz. his wife fifty pounds Sterl. to be deposited in the hands of Mr. Micajah Perry of London Merchant for their use to be paid to them when or age or married or to the survivor of them. It. I give to Mary Jarrett the sister of John Jarrett twenty five pounds Sterl. to be paid her within two years after my decease. It. I give to Henry Jenkins the son of Capt. Henry Jenkins my saddle horse I had of Mr. John Waugh

with my best saddle bridle pistoll and holster. It. I give my Divinity books to my Loving wife Rachel desiring her to give Such of them as Shee shall see fitt to Mr. Joseph Pettitt all my history bookes. I give Johannah the wife of John Jarrett all my Law bookes, I give to Wm. Edwards and Dionisius Wright to be equally divided between them. It. I give to his Ex:y Sir Edward Andros Knt. Gov'r. etc. forty shill. Sterl. to buy him a ring and to my good friend William Davis and Capt. Arthur Spicer forty shill. each to buy them a ring and I give ten pounds Sterl. to be disposed of by my Loving wife Rachell in mourning rings to such persons as she shall see fitt. It. I give to my Loving friend Wm. Edwards ... the Land he now useth without my garden pailes Joining to his Land and the said Land within a Line to be run from the Southeast end of my garden pailes till it come opposite to the Ditch of Mr. James Chudleighs orchard and from thence by a Line to the said Ditch ... It. It is my will that my Indian woman Dorothy Jubille be free Immediately after my decease being satisfied she is no slave and in full of corn and clothes I give her fifty shill. Sterl. It. It is my will that Captain Henry Jenkins have the goods I bought of Capt. Tolbett ... It. I give to Mary Anterbus(?) ye sum of ten pdd. Sterl. ... where she shall be free in full of her freedom corn and clothes ... It. I give to my Loving wife Rachell my personall Estate during her natural Life and after her decease I give the same to my very goods friends William Edwards and Capt. George Marable and Mr. John Wright or any two of them to take an Inventory of my said personall Estate ... It. I give to my Loving wife Rachel all my Lands & houses ... and after her decease I give the same to Jeffery Jefferys Esq. ... Debts ... Lastly I do hereby constitute and appoint my Loving wife Rachell my full and Sole Ex'x and I desire my good friends Mr. Edwards Capt. Geo. Marable and Mr. Dionisius Wright to be overseers ... (they to be executors after wife's decease) ... It. I give to John Jarrett such of my wearing apparell ... 18 Aug. 1697.
Wit.: Wm. Ayleth   Signed Wm. Sherwood
    James Jessell   Jas. City Co., 7 Feb. 1697, proved by
    Geo. Williams   oaths of all the Wit.
    Cope Doyley   Test Robt. Beverley Cl. Cur.

Ms. # 66.

This Deed Indented & made, Between George Hughes & Ann his wife of James Citty County on the one part, and James Whaley of Bruton parish in York County on the other part ... two young negroes (Vizt.) a male & a female aged between 16 & 18 years old and 10 li. Sterl. paid by ye sd. James Whaley, 250 Acres, James City Co., according to Mr. Lewis's Survey, said 250 Acres Joyning & bounded W: 245 Perches, thence ... on ye Hoppole Swamp to ye place where it first began: 50 Acres of which divident or Tract of Land being formerly sold to Ralph Tuskin by Richard Wardey ... 14 Nov. 1698.
Wit.: Joseph ED Daws Mark   Signed with   George Hughes
    Lazarus S Thomas his Mark   seals.   Ann Hughes.
    Alex. Ebonyman.   Court Jas. City Co., 6 Dec. 1698.
     Test C: C: Thacker Cl Cur.

Ms. # 67.

I John Jarrett of James Citty in ye County of James Citty Gent: ... paid by John Howard of ye same place & County ... sell ... unto ye sd. John Howard 28½ Acres, beginning on James River at ye head of a great Slash Issuing into the back river & down ye sd. Slash Ea: ½ point ... to ye back river marsh & up ye same to a marked Persimon tree under block hill point thence under ye sd. hill west 6 cha: to James River and down ye sd. river to ye first mentioned Slash includeing 8 Acres, 43 cha: to ye land formerly belonging to Rich'd James and along it South 23 cha: to a branch of Pitch & Tarr Swamp thence up ye sd. branch to James River, and up ye River to ye first mentioned place it began, which land (saving and excepting two Acres of Land or thereabouts is lately in ye possession of ffrancis Bullivant which was formerly leased unto John Hopkins for their lives, by Wm. Sherwood Gent: late deceased) was given and granted unto ye sd. John Jarrett by deed 30 Dec. 1693 by ye sd. Dec'd relacon ...

9 Feb. 1699.   Sealed & Signed Jn. Jarrett.
Wit.: John Young   Rec. Court, Jas. City Co., 6 May 1700.
                            Test C: C: Thacker Cl Cur.

Ms. # 68.

Land, James City Co., 27 Acres, late in possession of Jane Perkins, dec'd., is lately found to Escheat ... Inquisition ... John Lightfoot Esq., Escheator of the sd. County ... year 1700 ... grant unto Wm. Woodward of as. City Co., 28 Oct. 1702.

Ms. # 69.

Land Grant to Giles Webb, 1797 Acres, County of Henrico and on the North side of James River at a corner black oak belonging to the Land of Mr. Robert Beverley standing on Lower Westham Creek & thence on the said Beverleys Line North East by North 540 po: to his corner black oak thence West 414 po: crossing a branch of Lower Westham Creek to a Corner white oak thence South West crossing the Main branch of Lower Westham Creek... thence South ... thence West South West ... thence North West & by West 14 po: to a black oak belonging to the Land of Coll. Randolph, thence on his Line Southwest & by South 200 po: to a pohiccory and South 3 deg: West 208 po: to Tuchahow Creek: thence down Tuchahow Creek and James River as they wind and bend, to the mouth of Lower Westham Creek and thence up that Creek as it trendeth to the place we begun ... The said Land being due the said Giles Webb ... transportation of 36 pers. (names not given).
28 Oct. 1702   Signed ffra. Nicholson.

Ms. # 70.

Land Patent to Giles Webb, 1797 Acres, Henrico County, North side of James River at a place known by ye Name of Westham (description given as above) 28 Oct. 1702.
E Jennings Sec.   ffra. Micholson

Ms. # 71.

Survey of 25 Acres of Land to Wm. Sherwood, Platt given. 10 Dec. 1702, formerly belonging to Jane Perkins, Surveyed and set forth for William Woodward.

Ms. # 72.

In the Name of God Amen I William Broadribb, of James City County ... First ... debts ... Item I do give unto my son Benj. Brodribb after the death of my Loveing wife Lydia Brodribb my plantation whereon I now live & the land bounded as followeth beginning at ye mouth of the spring branch before the Door & up that branch to ye devideing of it & from the fork of the sd. branch up the middle of the point straight up the Maine road & downe the sd. Maine Road till it meets with Wormley's line at thickett of trees between the sd. Wormleys old feild & mine, by the Schoole house & downe that same Lane till it meet with the Line between Wm. Baylys land & mine & along that same line till it comes to Powhatan Swamp & then up the said Swamp to the mouth of the sd. br(-) where it began (Excepting the land whereon the _chooe (-) now standeth with half an acre of Land & firewood of my Land, I do give for the use of a School forever. I do give to my sd son Benj:a my plantation & lands as above (Excepting what is before excepted) to him & the heires of his Body ... Item I do give unto my son Wm. Brodribb at ye age of Eighteen years all the land whereon Lawrence Usher now liveth ... I give to my sd. Son William all my Land between the road that leads between Coll. Ludwells Mill & Powhatan Mill all ye Land between that Road & ye Line between Mr. Benj: Eggleston's land & mine (Excepting one acre of Land for the use of the Mill to him ...) Item I give unto my Son Abraham Brodribb at the age of Eighteen years all my land beyond the Maine road & all that I have beyond the Drinking Swamp branch Except in my Patent all but what is already disposed of ... Item I give unto my Son Thomas

Broadribb at age of Eighteen years all my land lying between the bounds of my Son Benjamins land & the bounds of my son Wm.'s land ... cononly called Purters Hill ... Item I do appoint ... friends Mr. Wm. Drumond Capt:n Marable & Mr. Benj. Eggleston or either two of them with my Loveing wife trustees to sell & dispose of my Land & plantation whereon Emanuell Dees now liveth & the produce of it I bequeath equally between my Son Thomas Broadribb & my two daughters to wit Susan & Lydia . Item I give My Mill & an Acre of Land to be divided amonst all my children (as they attain to the age of 18) (Vizt. to Benj. Broadribb Will Broadribb Susan Broadribb Thomas Broadribb & Lydia Broadribb & considering the many shares in the sd. Mill & for fear of their Disagreement I do appoint my two sons Benj. & William) who will be both of age before Mr. John Tulit his Lease of the said Mill be Expired that if they think it best when Mr. Tullit lease be out ... to sell the said mill & the produce of the sd. Mill I do give to be Equally divided amongst all my before named six children. Item I do give all my personall Estate to be Equally divided ... wife Lydia ... and ... six children. Lastly I do constitute and appoint my Loveing wife Lydia Broadribb whole & sole Executrix ...

Wit.: William W Wager his Mark   Signed Will Broadribb
      John Spratley   Court, Jas. City Co.,
      Eliz E Spratley her Mark.   17 June 1703, proved.

Ms. # 73.

Indenture, 11 Dec. 1704, Between S:r Jeffrey Jeffreys Knight Alderman of the City of London of the one part and Edward Jacquelyn of James Citty in the province of Virginia Merchant of the other part ... 5 s. by Edward Jaquelyn ... sold ... unto the said Edward Jaquelyn ... plantation ... in the possession of William Sherwood Gent. and now of the said Edward Jaquelyn, 400 acres, Jas. City Island and Jas. City Co. ... Wit.: R Beverley, Nath:ll Burwell, Rich'd Cocke Jun., Jn. Kinson(?), Leo Tarent, Ja: Benough. Court, Jas. City Co., 6 April 1706, Deed of Lease proved by oaths of Richard Cocke & Robt. Beverley.

Ms. # 74.

Marguritte Lady Culpeper Thomas Lord Fairfax and Catherine his wife proprietors of the Northern Neck ... Robert Carter Jun:r. son of Robert Carter Esq. of the County of Lancaster ... Ten Acres and Thirty seven poles, County of Stafford ... Thomas Gregg Surveyor ... unto Robert Carter Junior ... and for want of such heirs to Charles Carter brother of ye s:d Robert ... and for want of such heirs to John Carter Eldest Son of ye s:d Robert Carter Esq. ... County of Stafford afores:d on ye North side of Occoquan River a little below ye falls thereof and Bounded according to ye s:d survey as followeth: Vizt Beginning at a marked Red Oake standing at ye mouth of a Gutt or small Branch of ye s:d River & on ye upper side thereof & Extends No-th ... to a markt Chesnutt Oake on ye s:d Branch Side then North ... to a Markt Hickory, Then North ... to a Markt Ewe Tree standing on ye East side of another small branch then down ye branch to ye River South ... Then to ye beginning South ... given at our office in Lancast:r County w:thin our sd. Proprietary ... 10 Oct. 1707. Tho: Hooper, Cl. of ye Propriet:rs office. Signed Robert Carter.

Ms. # 77 (numbered in the Mss. as such)

Indenture, 7 July 1707 between John Tullit of the County of Henrico of the one part and Phillip Ludwell of the County of James City Esq. of the other part Witnesseth that whereas the said John Tullit is now Lawfully possest of 25 acres, Jas. City Co., & Parish of James City, late in the tenure and occupation of Thomas Middleton and of 76 acres in the same parish and County late in the tenure and occupation of Henry Jenkins or William Forrester or one of them and 75 acres in the same parish and County Lying upon Poetan Swamp near Poetan Mill, lately in the possession of William Pussan(?) ... and one Plantation in James Town Island Commonly called Goose Hill by virtue of a Lease for the same from John Hopkins, 2 Jan. 1702 for 20 years

from that date under the rent of 40 s. a year ... also of one Water
Mill and certain lands adjoining lying in the said County and parrish
of James City by virtue of a Lease for the same from William Broadrib
dec'd., 8 Jan. 1696, term of 20 years from 1 Nov. last past, rent of
3000 lbs. Tob. a year that term; now the said John Tullet, for 100
li. sterl. acknowledges every part thereof...

Wit.: Cha: Chiswell   Signed &   John IT Tullitt
       John Baird   sealed.

Court, Jas. City Co., 7 July 1707, Adm. to Rec. Test. Wil Robertson
Cl Cur.

Ms. #78.

Indenture, 6 June 1708, Between Major George Marable Mr. Benjamin
Mr. Christopher Smith & Liddya his wife trustees of William Broadribb
Gent. Late of James City Dec'd. of the one part & Joseph Chemerson of
the County aforesaid of the other part whereas William Broadribb: By
his Last Will & Testament, 3 May 1703... Christopher Smith & Liddia
his wife then wife of ye said Testat:r...Sold ... unto the said Joseph
Chermesion ... the sd. Land being formerly granted ... by Pattent, 5
June 1654, 24 acres to Anthony Coleman, assigned to Jno. ffitchet & by
him assigned to John Phips & Wm. Harris & by Sd. Phipps assigned his
right & share to ye sd. Major Morrison.

Wit.: W.(?) Lightfoot   Signatures with seals; seals   Geo: Marable
       Wm. Trayser   have paper strips over them   Bena: Eggleston
                          for protection.   Chris:r Smith
                                                         Lydia Smith

Court, Jas. City, 6 June 1709. Adm. to Rec. Test. Wil. Robertson
Cl Cur.

Mss. # 79 & 80. & 81

In the Name of God Amen I William Randolph of Turkey Island in
the County & Parish of Henrico in James River in Dig:y Gent. being in
60th year of my age ... wife Mary Randolph during her natural life the
plantation I now live on, 200 & odd acres, part of 1000 Acres called
Turkey Island ... After her death I give and devise the said Plantation and all the Houses ... to my Son W:m Randolph ... I give and
devise to my said Dear wife Mary Randolph & her Heirs for ever, my
share of Martins Swamp and the Acre of ground in the Town of Bermuda
Hundred which I have entered for stoping the will given her Land in
the Neck with the s:t part of the Swamp & the acre of ground in the
Town to one of my sons if he should Live upon the sd. Acre of ground in
the Town aofresd. I give and devise all my Land ... including in my
Patent of Curles ... lying on both sides of Poplar Brook to my sons
Isham and Thom:s. Randolph, about 750 acres ... my son Isham in proba-
bility will not settle in Virg:a ... I give and devise to my sons
Rich'd. & John all my three tracts of land ... purchased of John
Woodson Samuel Shnibb and John Morton ... upon Chickahomy Swamp,
about 900 acres ... I give and devise to my son Edward Randolph ...
upon Chickahominy, adj. Mr. James Cocke & Joseph Watson, 625 Acres ...
bought of Mr. Tho. Cocke dec'd. ... I give and devise all my lands
between land given to my son William above Westham upper creek &
Tuchahoe Creek, being 3256 acres I purchased of Edmund Jennings Esq. to
be equally divided between my sons Isham, Thos., Rich'd., John &
Edward ... I give and devise my upper Island lying in James River as
afd. to be Equally divided between my three sons Thos., Rich'd.,
& John ... I give & devise my land upon the North side of James River
w:ch lyes above Tuchahoe Creek, part of my Patent w:ch I have for the
Islands ... unto my son Edward Randolph ... I do hereby allot and
appoint my land & Plantation at Sigeon Swamp, Surry Co., between 1000
& 1100 acres ... and 10 negroes (named) ... for the use of Mr. Micajah
Parry & Comp:y mercht. in London ... satisfy what I may owe them,
until the same be fully paid & I desire my Sons Henry and Thos.
Randolph to take care, etc. ... negroes and all the stock aforesaid
to be equally divided between my said two sons ... I give and bequeath
to my Loving wife Mary ... bed, etc., ... negro man Ned my negro
woman Sarah & her children (named) ... I give and bequeath to my
Daughter Stith & my Daughter Bland each of them a ring ... I do hereby

nominate & appoint my aforesd. wife & my sons Willia, Henry & Thos. Randolph Ex'ors ...
6 Mar. 1709
Wit.: Rich'd. Dennis   Signed Wm. Randolph
       Henry Randolph   Proved 8/13 (no year given)
       T. Eldridge   Test Wm. Randolph
                          A Copy Fortu. Sydnor DC

Ms. # 82.

Indenture, 6 May 1710, Between John Howard of Jas. City Co., Taylor, of the one part & John Baird of the same Co., Carpenter, of the other part ... sold 172 perches in James City in the County aforesaid bounded from the North East Corner of the Church yard along the railes thereof North ... to the hon:ble Nathaniel Bacon Esq. his land and along it North ... to the great old road and along the same to the first mentioned corner ... and also 28½ acres, James City Island, beginning on James River at the head of a great slash issuing into the back river and Southerly ... Easterly to the back river marsh and up the same to a marked persimon tree under block house hill point thence under the said hill west 6 cha: to James River and down the said river to the first mentioned slash including 8 acres and thence agains down the said slash 43 cha: to the land formerly belonging to Richard James and along it South 23 cha: to a branch of Pitch & Tarr Swamp thence up the said branch to James river and up the River to the place it begun.
Wit.: Phill: Ludwell   Signed, probably   John IH Howard
      John Clayton   with seal
Court, Jas. City Co., 6 May 1710, Adm. to Rec., Test. Wil. Robertson.

Ms. # 83.

I John Barber, received 10,000 li Tob. of Thomas Rably ... sell .. Land my dec'd ffather Jno. Barber loved on in James Citty, bounded on ye east by Mr. Holders Land on ye North with Major White & Newell & on ye West on Holliday & on ye South upon ye River, being ¼ of an acre ... 7 ffeb. 1677/8.
Wit.: John Stith   Signed & probably   John Barber.
      Edward Sanderson once sealed.
  23 April 1678, Acknowledged in Court & Recorded.
  Test Henry Hartwell Cl Cur.

Ms. # 84.

Survey, 27 May 1712, for the hon:ble Phillip Ludwell Esq., one tract of Governors Land, 102 Acres in the Maine, James City Co., bounded Vizt. beginning at a corner cyprus on James River and running along the free land of Coll. Ludwell North ... thence a long an old ditch ... to a slash at the end of the sd. ditch, thence along a slash dividing this from the land of the sd. Coll. Ludwell North ... thence to James town main Road thence up it North ... thence along an old road that went to Major Marable North ... thence along an old dividing line dividing this from Major Marables North ... to a gum standing on the North side of a slash thence North ... to two stakes drove into an old stump, thence South ... to a stake by James town main road, thence along an old ditch South ... to a gum near the head of the Northerly branch of a small swamp, thence down the Northerly branch of the sd. Swamp to the Westerly head, thereof to the end of an old ditch thence along it South ... to the river side thence along it to the place began at.
Signed   Simon Jeffreys Surveyor J:C:C:

Ms. # 85.

Platt: Survey, 15 June 1712, for the Honu:ble Phillip Ludwell Esq., 102 Acres for himself and 235 for Wm. Drummond, lying & being in the Main in Jas. City Co. The Platt is given. Signed Simon Jeffreys, Sur., J.C.C.

Ms. # 86.

Platt, 102 acres of Governors land, in the Main, Jas. City Co., for Philip Ludwell Esq., 27 May 1712; Platt given. Signed by same surveyor.

Ms. # 87.

Indenture, 20 July 1713 between Isham Randolph of the one part & William Randolph of the other part, for 5 shillings by William Randolph ... sold unto ye sd. William Randolph ... two tracts of Land, 580 Acres & 500 Acres, above Upper Westham Creek on ye North side of James River and the other, 80 Acres is a part of an Island lying above ye sd. Creek, upon James River, on ye North side thereof & known by ye name of Lower Tuckahoe Island, w:ch sd. Land was devised to ye sd. Isham Randolph by ye Last Will & testament of his dec'd. father William Randolph.
Wit.: William Finney   Signed & probably   Isham Randolph
      Jos. Royall Junr.   once sealed
      Thomas Randolph   Court at Verina for Henrico County,
      Rich'd. Randolph   3 Aug. 1713, Admitted to Record.
      Henry Randolph Junr.   Test. William Randolph Cl Cur.
      Jno. Randolph

Ms. # 87, A.

Indenture, 21 July 1713, between Isham Randolph of the one part & William Randolph of the other part (& the recitation of the earlier Indenture), for 25 pounds Sterl. to Isham Randolph by William Randolph ... granted, etc. ...
Wit.: Same as above   Signed with seal.   Isham Randolph
On the other side: Court at Verina for Henrico Co., 3 April 1713,
  Admitted to Record.   Tests. William Randolph Cl Cur.

Ms. 88.

Indenture, 2 Aug. 1713 between Fras. Lightfoot, of Jas. City Co., of one part & Thomas Randolph of Henrico Co., of the other part ... 3256 Acres, Henrico Co., for 30 pounds Sterl. granted, etc...unto Thomas Randolph.
Wit.: Tho. Eldridge   Signed Fran. Lightfoot
      Philip Lightfoot   Court at Varina for Henrico Co., 3 Aug.
      Thos. Bouth   1713, Adm. to Rec. To Wit Wm. Randolph.
      A copy: Fortu. Sydnor Dcl.

This Indenture, 2 Aug. 1713, Same Parties, 5 shillings ... sold ... 3256 Acres ... Bounded as followeth (Vizt.) Beginning at a great white oak where Tuckahoe Creek forces Between the Isles, and Falls into the River thence running according to the meanders of the said Creek North ... to a corner gum on Tuckahoe Creek side thence North ... to a corner ash that stands on Tuchahoe Island Creek side thence up the said Creek to the place begun at.
Wit.: Same as above. Same signature and recording, but no copy named.

Ms. # 89.

Indenture, 7 Nov. 1714, between John Randolph of the one part & William Randolph of the other part, for 5 pounds Sterl., granted, etc., tp William Randolph, Co. & parish of Henrico, North side of James River, above Upper Westham Creek, 500 Acres, Devised to the said John by the last will & Testament of his dec'd. father.
Wit.: Thos. Randolph   Signed   Jno. Randolph
      Rich'd. Randolph   Henrico Co., June Court 1779(?), Adm. to
      Henry Randolph   Rec.
      Rene La force   Copy by William White Clk. H. Court.

William Randolph of Par. of Hen. Co., Gent. ... my son William Randolph, of same, granted two parcels of Tracts of Land, Westham on

24

the North side of James River, Co. aforesd. beginning at a great red oak upon Horsepen run & running for this breadth up my land ... to the back line of Colo. Jennings his Pattent of which Pattent my Land is the one half then Down the said Back Line of the Pattent to the Lower Most Corner Tree of the same & then down the other. Line of the said Pattent to the place begun at ... 542 acres ... also half of my Lower land ... 80 Acres ... by virtue of a conveyance from Colo. Edmund Jennings, 28 April 1690.
Wit.: Step. Sareazin   Signed Wm. Randolph
   Jn I Morton his mark.
  Ack. in open Court, Test James Cocke Clk. Court
  A Copy by Wm. White   Clk. H. Court.

Ms. # 90.

Indenture, 11 Sept. 1715, Between Mary Whaley of York Co., of the one part & Henry Cary Junr. of James City Co., of the other part ... sold ... unto the said Henry ... 100 Acres, part of 200 acres, which was sold by John Phipps and Mary Phipps unto Otho Thorp, Co. of Jas. City, ...
Wit.: Edward Jaquelin   Signed &   Mary Whaley
   Jno. Sclater   sealed.
  Court, Jas. City Co., 12 Sept. 1715, Adm. to Rec.
   Test Wil. Robertson Cl Cur.

Ms. # 91.

Indenture, 12 Sept. 1715, Between Mary Whaley & Henry Cary (as above) for 20 pounds Sterl. to be paid on the last day of Dec. 1716 also the same 1717, 1718 & 1719, the said Mary has granted ... sold ... 100 Acres which was formerly sold by John Phipps & Mary Phipps unto Otho Thorp and is bounded by the land of Mr. Richard Bland lately bought of the said Mary and the lands of Mr. Mongo Ingles Mr. Nath. Crawly Capt. Timson and Mathew Hall.
Wit.: Same as above   Signed Mary Whaley
  Court, Jas. City Co., 12 Sept. 1715, Adm. to Rec.
   Test. Wil. Robertson Cl Cur.

Ms. # 92.

Indenture, 13 Jan. 1717, Between John Baird, Jas. City Co., Carpenter, of the one part & Edward Travis, of the same Co., Gent., of the other part, for 30 pounds Sterling to Edward Travis ... sold ... 172 perches in James City, & In Co. aforesaid, bounded (description as given before).
Wit.: Robert Cole   Signed & probably   John Baird
   Thomas Cole.   once sealed
  Court, Jas. City Co., 13 Jan. 1717, Adm. to Rec.
  Test Wil. Robertson Cl Cur.

Ms. # 93.

(The right corner is torn.) I Margaret (- & see signature) P/A to Wil. Robertson, Right of Dower in land sold by my said Husband John Blair to Edward Travis lying in James City in the County aforesaid
Wit.: Wm. Frayser   Signed & probably   Margaret Baird
   Tho. Cole   once sealed

Ms. # 94.

Indenture, 2 Jan. 1718, Between Richard Randolph, of one part & William Randolph of other part, for 3 pounds Sterling hath granted etc., to Wm. Randolph land in Co. & parish of Henrico, on North side (of) James River, above Upper Westham Creek, 500 Acres, It being devised to the said Richard by the Last Will & Testament of his dec'd father.   Signed   Rich'd Randolph
Wit.: Joseph Pleasants   Henrico Co., Jan. Court 1718, Adm. to Rec.
   John Watson   A Copy   J Berkley D Clk.
   Charles Ballow

Ms. # 95.

Indenture, 2 Jan. 1718, Between Thomas Randolph, of one part & William Randolph, of the other part, for 3 pounds Sterl. hathe granted etc. to Wm. Randolph, Land in Co. & Parish of Henrico on the North side of James River above Upper Westham Creek, 500 Acres, it being devised to the sd. Thomas by the Last Will & Testament of his dec'd father.

Wit.: Joseph Pleasants
     John Watson
     Charles Ballow

Signed Thos. Randolph.
Hen. Co., Jan. Court 1718, Adm. to Rec.
H. Wood Clk Cur.

Ms. # 96 & 97

To Robert Bolling, William Stark, Theophilus Field, Hugh Miller and Samuel Gordon, Gentlemen, Whereas William Broadnax late of Jas. City Co., Gent., now of the County of Prince George and Anne his wife by their certain Indenture of ffeoffment, 1 Jan. 1710 conveyed unto Christopher Perkins of Norfolk Co., Gent. the fee simple Estate of several tracts or parcels of Land and Lots in Parish of James City, in Co. of Jas. City ... give unto you or any two of you Power to receive the acknowledgement which the said Anne shall be willing to make before you of the conveyance aforesaid in the said Indenture which is hereunto annexed ... 17 Jan., 8 year of reign of Geo. II.
                                  Signed Ben: Waller.
Commission, Prince George, to Robert Bolling & Samuel Gordon, Anne Broadnax examined, and certified by the within named justices, 1 Feb. 1744/5.

Ms. # 98.

Indenture, 1 Jan 1744 Between William Broadnax of Jas. City Co., Gent. and Anne his wife of the one part & Christopher Perkins of Co. of Norfolk, Gent., of the other part, for 541 pounds, 13 shillings, current money of Virginia ... sold ... Land ... in Island of Jas. City Co. of Jas City, 127 Acres & 7/10 parts of an Acre, and bounded as follows (that is to say) Beginning on James River at a Ditch adjoining to the Market Place in James Town, thence North ... to the Garden Pales of Richard Ambler Esq. (formerly Edward Jacquelin) thence South ... to Three Mulberry Trees marked inwards at the End of a Double Ditch, thence along the said last mentioned Ditch Southwardly ... to a Gum Tree, on the Edge of Pitch and Tar Swamp, thence South ... to a corner Stake between Edward Champion Travis and Richard Ambler (formerly between the said Travis and the aforesaid Edward Jacquelin) thence South ... to a stake at the Head of a Marsh, thence along the said Marsh to a Bridge over the same, thence South ... to the head of a small Gut making out of Parchmores Creek, thence down the said Gut to the mouth thereof, thence up the said Creek to the Fork, thence South to James River aforesaid, and thence up the said River to the Beginning ... being in the said Island of James City, commonly called and known by the name of Thorney Ridge, 12 Acres, which William Broadnax purchased of John Green, 5 & 6 days of Dec. 1712, made between John Green and Anne his wife of the one part, and William Broadnax the Father of the other part ... other parcel of Land, Island of Jas. Town, Co. of Jas. City, 107 Acres, which William Broadnax by Indenture, 22 April 1736, made between Francis Bullivant, Co. of Jas. City, planter of the one part & William Broadnax, of the other part; also Tract or parcel of Land, Island of Jas. Town, Co. of Jas. City, 28½ Acres, by Indenture, 17 July 1719 between Edward Travis, Gent., Jas. City Island & Co. of Jas. City, of one part & William Broadnax the Father; also 3 Acres, one Rood & 6 Poles, Island of James Town, Co. of Jas. City, by Letters Patent 16 Oct. 1694 to Robert Beverley, who by Deed of Lease and Release, 8 May 1718 between Robt. Beverley of King & Queen Co., Gent., & William Broadnax the Father; also 172 perches, Island of Jas. Town, Co. of Jas. City, by Letters Patent, 20 April 1694, to John Howard; also 3 Lots or Parcels of Land, Island of Jas. City, Co. of Jas. City, where the Ferry is now kept from James Towne aforesaid, which were devised to the said William Broadnax (Party to these Presents) by the last Will & Testament of one

Edward Ross, dec'd.
No Witnesses   Signed and   W. Brodnax
                    2 seales.   Ann Brodnax
(The text contains several spellings: Broadnax, Broadnox, Brodnax.)
1 Jan. 1744, a memof Sale. Court, Jas. City Co., 14 Jan. 1744, Adm. to Rec. Test. Ben: Waller.

Ms. # 99.

     I Phillip Ludwell of Jas. City Co., Esq. for 25 pounds, current money of Va., paid by Edward Jaquelin, of Jas. City ... sold ... said Edward Jaquelin, 27 Acres in Jas. City Main, by patent 28 Oct. 1702 to William Woodward & by him conveyed to John Tullett and by the said Tullett sold and conveyed to me ... 9 June 1718.
No Witnesses   Signed & probably   Phill: Ludwell.
                 once sealed.

Ms. # 100.

     Inquisition, Jas. City Co., 21 Nov. 1720, Edmund Jennings, Esq., Escheator of said Co.; It appears that Ralph Tuftain late of the said Jas. City Co. dyed seized of 50 Acres ... Escheat ... said Ralph Tuftian which land upon a Survye, 21 Dec. 1721 by Christopher Jackson Surveyor of the said Co., containing 50 Acres, and Whereas Robert Ashurst of the said County ... granted ... unto Robert Ashurst ... the said 50 Acres, bounded as followeth: to wit, Beginning at a Saplin red oak and running from thence North ... to a Sallow near the said Ashursts Spring thence down the said Spring Branch according to the meanders thereof till it meets with the main run of Powhatan Swamp thence up Powhatan Swamp according to the meanders thereof to a white oak being a corner tree between this land and Benjamin Picketts land thence along the line dividing this land from Benjamin Picketts, South ... to a Sallow being a marked (worn) __ said line and now made a corner of the said Ashursts land from thence. North 78 deg: West (worn) 94 po: to the beginning ... 22 June 1722.

Ms. # 101.

     Micajah Perry of London Merchant and John Clayton of Williamsburg in Va., Esq., Whereas Micajah in writing, Letter of Attorney, 6 Nov. 1710, did authorize the said John Clayton ... to Bargain Sele etc. ... all such lands ... now for 5 pounds of Lawful money of Gr. Britain by Edward Jaquelin of James City in Jas. City Co., Gent., Messuage or Tenament and half an acre in James City, Jas. City Co., formerly in possession of John Jarrett dec'd., and bounded on the South by the River James East on the Old ffort North on the Land where the Mansion house of the said Edward Jaquelin now stands and West on the Land late in the Possession of William Marable ... 9 Sept. 1721.
No Witnesses.   Signed with   Micajah Perry
                 seal
   Court, Jas. City Co., 1 Sept. 1721, Adm. to Rec.
     Test Michl: Archer Cl Cur.

Ms. # 102.

     For 5 shillings, unto Mrs. Mary Whaley, Marsh land, on Queens Creek in York County, adjoining to a Tract of Land belonging to the said Mary Whaley & bounded as followeth to Wit Beginning - (near or next?) to the Capitol Landing Thence North ... down the said Creek to a Gut Thence South ... to the Beginning ... 21 Feb. 1725.

Ms. # 103.

     Indenture, 26 July 1743, between the Honorable William Gooch Esq. ... of the one part & Richard Ambler of York Town in the Parish of York Hampton & Co. of the other part, of York Co., Gent., Whereas the Trasurer & Company of Mine Adventurers and Planters of the City of London for the first Colony of Virginia by their Commission to Capt. George Yeardley, 18 Nov. 1618, 3000 Acres of Land ... Territory

of James Town in Va. & near Adjoining the said Town to be the seat and Land of Governor of Va. ... called by the Name of Governors Land ... Lands conquered or purchased of the Paspeheies and of other grounds next adjoining which said Land afterwards on or about the year 1625 was laid out and Surveyed by William Claybourn Esq. then Surveyor General of Va. ... granted ... to the said Richard Ambler ... Tract of Land being 110 acres ... 102 acres whereof was lately occupied by Philip Ludwell Esq. and 8 acres by Edward Ross and since by Edward Jaquelin late of James City Gent., dec'd., being part of the said 3000 acres called the Governors Land, in Parish & Co. Jas. City.
Wit.: Anne Staunton   Signed with   William Gooch.
Nath: Walthor   seal
    Endorsement: Governor's Lease for 102 Acres which Mr. Jaquelin bought of Col. Ludwell Anno 1712 & 8 Acres w:ch he bought of Edward Ross. 110 Acres.

Ms. # 104.

Indenture, 6 Feb. 1744, Between the Hon. William Gooch, Esq. of one part & William Wager Junr. of Jas. City of the other, Whereas the Treasurer (etc., as above) ... 122 acres lately in the Possession of Edward Jaquelin being part of 3000 Acres called the Governors Land, Parish & Co. of Jas. City.
Wit.: Anne Staunton Signed & probably, sealed: Will Gooch.
                Signature only: Wm: Wager Junr.
    For sum of 80 pounds Cur:t Money ... Lease ... to Thomas Holt of Jas. City Co., signed Christopher Ford Jur., 26 Nov. 1756. Wit: Benjamin Bryan & Ben: Waller.
    For sum of 150 pounds Cur:t Money ..... to James Heart of the City of Williamsburg ... 20 June 1762.
Wit: John Moore   Signed &   Tho. Holt.
    William Maye   once sealed.
    12 June 1762, Rec'd of Mr. James Heart the above sum & signed Tho: Holt.
    For sum of 150 pounds Cur:t Money ... to John Ambler of James City.
Wit.: Ro. Higginson   Signed &   James Heart.
    Edward Wilkinson   sealed.

Ms. # 105.

I William Broadnox of Pr. Geo. Co., Gent., for 30 pounds paid by Christopher Perkins of Jas. City Co., Gent., one negro man slave named William Leverpool ... 13 Feb. 1744.
Wit.: Thomas Broadribb   Signed W. Brodnax.
    Benjamin Broadribb
    Memo: 1 Jan. 1745/6 for 30 pounds Chr. Perkins assigns his right & title in the bill to Richard Ambler.
Wit.: Wm. Cole   Signed   Chris:r Perkins.
    Charles Thompson.

Ms. # 106.

"Sold & conveyed to the said William Brodnax the Father the said last mentioned Lands by the Name of all his the said Roberts Houses and Land in James Town" ... also 122 Perches of Land, Island of Jas. City, bounded as by Patent, 2 April 1694, whereby the said Land was granted to one John Howard; also those Lots or parcels of Land, Island of Jas. City, where the Ferry is now kept from Jamestown aforesaid, which were devised to the said William Brodnax the Son by the last will & Testament of one Edward Ross dec'd., ... said Christopher Perkins (Party to these Presents) by Indenture of Feosment, 1 Jan. 1744, by the said William Brodnax the Son ... (all as in the Ms.)

Ms. # 107.

Indenture, 1 Jan. 1745, Between Christopher Perkins of Jas. City Co., Gent., and Elizabeth his wife of the one part & Richard Ambler of

the Town & Co. of York, Esq. of the other part, for 680 pounds Cur. money of Va. ... sold ... unto the said Richard Ambler in Island of James Town and Jas. City Co., 127 7/10 Acres as follows, that is to say, Beginning on James River at a Ditch adjoining to the Market Place in James Town, thence North ... to the Garden Pales of the said Ambler (formerly of Edward Jacquelin) thence South ... along the said Pales thence South ... to three Mulberry Trees marked inwards at the End of a double Ditch, thence along the said last mentioned Ditch Southwardly 15 3/4 cha: according to the meanders thereof, to a Gum Tree, thence South ... East 9 cha: to a Gum Tree on the Edge of Pitch and Tar Swamp thence South ... to a corner stake between Edward Champion Travis and the said Richard Ambler (formerly between the said Travis and the said Jaquelin) thence South ... to a Stake at the Head of a Marsh, thence along the said Marsh to a Bridge over the same, thence South 71 deg: East to the Head of a Small Gut making out of Parchmore's Creek, thence down the said gut to the mouth thereof thence up the said Creek to the Fork, thence South to James River aforesaid and thence up the said River to the Beginning. Also all that other Tract of Land, Island of James Town, Jas. City Co., commonly called and known by the Name of Thorny (worn Ridge, 12 Acres, which Wm. Brodnox dec'd. purchased of John Green, lease and release, 5 & 6 of Dec. 1712 and from the said William Brodnax descended and came to his son William Brodnax; also Tract or parcel of Land, Jas. Town Island, Jas. City Co., 107 Acres, which William Brodnax the Son by Indenture, 2 April 1736, between Francis Bullivant, of Jas. City Co., Planter of the one part & William Brodnax of Jas. City Co., Gent., of the other; also Tract or parcel of Land, Island of Jas. Town, Jas. City Co., 28½ acres, by Indenture, 17 July 1719, between Edward Travis, of Jas. City Island & Co., of the one part & William Brodnax the Father, of the same Co., Gent. of the other part; also 3 acres & 6 poles, Island of Jas. Town, Jas. City Co., by Patent, 6 Oct. 1694, to Robert Beverley & by deed 7 & 8 May 1718 between Robert Beverley of King & Queen Co., Gent., of one part & William Brodnax the Father of James City, Gent., on the other, for valuable consideration therein mentioned, --- (the Ms. ends here). The following is on this Ms.:
No   Signed with   Christopher Perkins
Witnesses.   seals.   Elizabeth Perkins.

Ms. # 108.

Indenture, 5 March 1745, between Robert Anderson of the Parish of St. Martin, Co. of Hanover Planter (Son of David Anderson late of King William Co., dec'd.) and Frances the wife of the said Robert Anderson, of the one part & Richard Ambler of the Town of York Esq., of the other, for 5 Shillings ... sold ... 400 acres & 100 acres, which descended unto the said Robert Anderson as eldest Son and Heir of his Father David Anderson dec'd.; 400 acres granted to David Anderson in his Life time by Patent at Williamsburg, 13 Nov. 1721, on the lower side of Taylor's Creek, Hanover County, Bounded as followeth to wit, Beginning at a Hiccory on the said Creek being the upper corner of a Survey made by Robert Jenings Thence along his Line North ... to a parcel of marked pines in the head of a valley that runs into Charles Swamp Thence down the Swamp by the Water Courses making upon a straight Line 320 po: to the mouth thereof Thence down the Creek by the Water Courses to the Beginning making upon a straight Line 308 po: the tract of 100 acres (which is contiguous to the other above mentioned Tract of 400 acres) was purchased by the above named David Anderson in his Life time of one William Morris recorded in Hanover Co., bounded as followeth, to wit, Beginning at the upper Line of the said William Morris running down the Creek to the first Swamp so up the Swamp to the back Line to the Head Line then to the place - (worn; probably the place it began).
Wit.: John Garland   Signed with   Robt. Anderson
       Barttelot Anderson   2 seales.   Frances Anderson
       Fran:s Smith

Ms. # 109.

 I Robert Anderson of the Parish of St. Martin, Ha. Co., Planter, (son of David Anderson late of King William Co., dec'd) bound to Richard Ambler of Town of York, 1000 pounds cur. money of Va., 6 March 1745: Condition, that Robert Anderson & Frances his wife, in Indenture of Release, date above.

Wit.: John Garland	Signed &	Robert Anderson
Bartelot Anderson	sealed.	Court, 5 June 1746, Adm. to Rec.
Fran. Smith		Test. Henry Robinson, Cl Cur.

Ms. 110

 Indenture, 6 March 1745, Between Robert Anderson of the Parish of St. Martin, Han. Co., Planter (Son of David Anderson late of County of King William dec'd) and Frances the wife of the said Robert Anderson of the one part & Richard Ambler of the Town of York, Esq., of the other, for 175 pounds cur. money of Va. ... sold ... 400 acres & 100 acres, descended to Robert Anderson as eldest son and Heir of his said Father David Anderson dec'd., the said 400 acres granted to David Anderson by Patent at Williamsburg, 13 Nov. 1721 (description as above).

Sam	Signed with	Robt. Anderson
Wit.	2 seals.	Frances Anderson.

 Rec'd f 175 0. 0., 6 March 1745, Robt. Anderson; wit. are the same At Court of Han. Co., 6 Mar. 1745, by Robert Anderson & Frances his wife (she privately examined). Acknowledged & Relase & receipt. Adm. to Rec. Test. Henry Robinson Cl Cur. Truly rec. & same Test.

Ms. # 111.

 For 40 Shillings, 390 Acres, Co. of Henrico, to Hatcher(?) Burton, Bounded as followeth, to Wit, Beginning at a corner white oak standing South side Westham Creek in Mr. Randolphs Line Thence on that Line South West up the Hill ... Thence on an old Line of the said Randolph's South ... to a corner black oak Thence on a new line North 76 po: to a Hiccory Thence North 42 deg: East over Honey(?) Hill 204 po: to two Spanish Oaks and a pine standing in the Fork of Westham Creek and from thence down the said Creek according to the Several meanders to the place it began at.

Ms. # 112.

 Indenture, 31 May 1747, Between the Rt. Hon. Sir William Gooch Baronet ... of the one part & William Nugent of the Parish and County of James City on the other, Whereas the Treasurer and Company of Adventurers and Planters of the City of London for the first Colony of Va. by their Commission to Capt. George Yardley, 18 Nov. 1618, 3000 acres, Jas. Town, adjoining the said Town, and of the Lands formerly conquered or purchased of the Paspeheies and other grounds next adjoyning & in year 1625 laid out and surveyed by William Clayburn Esq. Then Surveyor General of Va., Now this Indenture Witnesseth That the said William Gooch ... demise grant and to farm lett to the said William Nugent, 105 Acres, formerly granted to George Marable, Gent., dec'd., by lease, - Jan. 1723, for 422 acres, survey made by Simon Jefferys, Surveyor of Jas. City Co., year 1712.

Wit.: Will:m Wyatt	Signed & with	William Gooch
Peter Muttlow	2 seals.	Wm. Nugent

 On the other side: I Edw"d Champion Travis Executor of the last Will & Testament of William Nugent late of James City, County dec'd do hereby assign over to Richard Ambler the title of the Lease, 10 April 1750.
Wit.: John Whitby. Signed Edward Travis, Executor.

Ms. # 113.

 Indenture, 13 Aug. 1747 Between the Rt. Hon. S:r Wm. Gooch Baronet, of the one part & Benj: Marrable, of Parish and County of James City on the other, Whereas the Treasurer (as above) ... demised

granted and to farm letten ... To the said Benj:a Marrable ... 105 Acres ... formerly granted to George Marrable Gent. Dec'd by Lease , - Jan. 1723, for 422 acres, Survey by Simon Jefferys Surveyor of Jas. City Co., year 1712.
Wit.: William Dawson   Signed with   Benj:a Marrable
       Rich: Taliaferro   2 seals.   Will Gooch

Ms. # 114.

Indenture, 15 June 1753, Between William Drummond of Jas. City Co., on the one part & Edward Champion Travis of the same Co., Gent., on the other ... sold ... ½ an acre, in James Town, formerly granted by William Sherwood, Gent., of Jas. City, to John Harris, of the same, by deed, 11 May 1696 & Recorded Jas. City Co. 16 July dollowing, afterwards sold by said Harris to William Drummond, of Jas. City Co., Gent., Father of the aforesaid William Drummond, by deed 4 Nov. 1701 & recorded in Jas. City Co., 6 of same Month, Bounded, on Omoonees Land and running along on the South side of the Mulberry Trees 90 foot thence Northerly towards the Maine Road 40 Foot thence North-West near the said Maine Road to the corner of Omoonee's Land 100 Foot and so along the Line of Omoonee's Land to the Place or stake it first began.
Wit.: George Wythe   Signed & probably   Wm. Drummond.
       Wm. Norvell   once sealed.
       Robert Sanders.

Ms. # 115.

Indenture, 8 Oct. 1753, Between Edward Champion Travis of Jas. City Co., Gent., of one part & Richard Ambler of York Co., Esq., of the other part ... sold ... unto said Richard Ambler, in James Town, ½ Acre, formerly by William Sherwood to John Harris of the same, 11 May 1696 & rec. 6 July following & Harris to William Drummond, of Jas. City Co., Gent., by deed 4 Nov. 1701 & Rec. 6 of same Month, afterwards by deed by William Drummond the Son to Edward Champion Travis, 15 June 1753 & rec. 10 Sept. following; Beginning (same description).
No   Signed and probably   Edw'd C: Travis.
Wit.   one sealed.

Ms. # 116.

Indenture, 30 Dec. 1755, Richard Ambler to his Son Edward Ambler, during his natural life. One acre of land in James Town Island, bounded by Slash which separates it from the Ferry house Land and on the South by James River, on the North by the Main Road, and on the West by the Acre of Land lately conveyed to John Smith Gent.
No   Signed and probably   Rich'd Ambler.
Wit.   once sealed.
On the other side: Court, Jas. City Co., 8 March 1756, ordered to be Recorded. Test. Ben: Waller Cl Cur.

Ms. # 117.

Plan of the Town of Beverley, etc. (Divided into lots, numbered, and some with names. Places: James River and Westham Creek.)

Ms. # 118.

Virginia Port York River. Omnibus Christi fidelibus ad quos presentes Litua preveneuint nos ministri vechiqulium secenipiud Domini Georgiis tertu Regis in Portu Eboraci (Anglici York) Salutem cum navi cula nuncupator Betsey cujus nancleuis sub Deo est.
Pro Madiera et alia loca transmarina cum -(-?) storminibus in eodem mavicula a Protu pradicto jam parata est decedere stine est quod universalati vestu tenue praesutium innolepimus fidemque indubitalem facimus quod (Deo optimos maximo summer Laus hibuatur) in hac Colonia Virginia nulla pestio plager nee moileus aliauis periculisus aut contigious sous ad presens existit.

In cujus rei testimonicum sigillum qui(?) nostii fecimus datum in Virginia pradicta 1 Aprilis Anno salutis Christiana 1761 Annoque Regni primo Georgii tutii regis. (A copy)

Ms. 119.

George III, etc., to William Dudley and Harwood Jones, Gent., Whereas William Harwood and Mary his wife by Indenture, 23 April 1761, conveyed to William Warburton the Fee Simple Estate ... lying ... in the Parish & County of James City, 120 acres ... the said Mary cannot conveniently travel ... to make acknowledgment of the said conveyance, Wherefore We do give unto you power to receive the acknowledgment ... 24 April (1761).   Ben Waller
On the other side: Her examination ... 25 April 1761.
William Dudley
Harwood Jones

Ms. # 120.

Indenture, 23 April 1761, Between William Harwood of the County of Warwick and Mary his wife of the one part & William Warburton of the County of Jas. City of the other part, for 150 pounds of cur. money ... granted ... sold ... unto William Warburton Land in Jas. City Parish & Co., 120 Acres, bounded as followeth, to wit, Beginning on James River at a corner pine running down the same South ... to a great Creek thence up the several courses of the said Creek to licking Gut thence up the said Gut according to its several courses to a corner white Oak on a drain of the said Gut thence South ... to the beginning.
Wit.: Turner Henley   Signed and   Will: Harwood
       John Ruhin Ju:r(?) the seals covered   Mary Harwood
       Benj:a Morris   with slips of paper
       Harwood Jones.   for protection.
On the other side: Court, Jas. City Co., Adm. to Record.
Test. Ben: Waller Cl Cur.

Ms. # 121.

Indenture, 5 Jan. 1765, Between Robert Carter Nicholas of the City of Williamsburg Esq. and Anne his wife of the one part & Edward Ambler of the Town and County of York Esq. of the other part, for 1500 pounds Cur. Money of Va. ... sold ... unto the said Edward Ambler ... in County of Henrico above the Falls of James Rivers, and on the North side thereof, the whole Tract containing 3000 acres more or less, and is the Tract of Land commonly called and known by the name of Westham, which the said Robert Carter Nicholas lately purchased of the honourable William Byrd Esq.
Wit.: Edw'd Charlton   One signature,   Ro: C. Nicholas.
       William Dangerfield possibly a
       John Ambler   second, and
       Wilson-Miles Cary   with what once
       John Burwell   were 2 seals.
On the other side: Rec'd. this 5 Jan. 1764 of Mr. Edward Ambler, 1500 pounds. Signed Ro. C. Nicholas. Wit.: Edw'd Charlton, William Dangerfield, John Ambler
Gen'l Court at the Capital, 4 May 1765, ordered to be recorded. Test. Ben: Waller Cl Cur.

Ms. # 122.

Articles of Agreement, 5 Jan. 1765, Between Robert Carter Nicholas, etc., & Edward Ambler, etc., Whereas ... Tract of Land the said Robert lately purchased of the hon:ble William Byrd Esq. ... do covenant each with the other his Heirs and Assigns, that within twelve months from the date hereof at fartherest, they will at their Joint Expense place and constantly keep Thirty working Negroes on the said Land during the Term of Twenty years next ensuing ... It is further agreed that a sufficient number of stocks of every kind ... shall be provided ... It is further agreed that Robert and Edward shall have the joint management of the Plantation slaves, and everything thereto belonging

during their joint lives ... in case of death of either of them, that the sole management shall be in the Surviver ... It is further agreed if the said Robert and Edward shall jointly purchase any Land adjoining ... It is further agreed ... which the said Robert ... hath been put in purchasing and surveying the said Land ... the said Edward Ambler to an equal share ... at the Expiration of the aforesaid Term of Twenty years they ... to dispose of the said Land, etc.
Wit: the five (There are no signatures, but the Ms. is
    signatures above.   in poor condition & a signature of Edward
                                  Ambler is patched on.)

Ms. # 123.

In the Name of God Amen I Richard Ambler of the Town & Co. of York in Va. Merchant... I give my son Edward all those Negroe Slaves and their increase which were employed on my Plantation in Caroline Co. which plantation was lately sold to Coll. John Baylor being 37 slaves old and young. And I give him all the stocks of cattle houses sheep and Hogs and the plantation utensils. I give my son Edward all my Negroe Slaves & their increase which were employed on my Plantation on Taylor's Creek in Hanover Co. being 13 slaves old and young, etc.

I give my said son Edward and to his Heirs forever my Plantation Black Swamp in Warwick Co. and all my belabouring Slaves, etc.

I give my son Edward and his Heirs forever my dwelling house whereon I now live, etc.

I give my son John one acre of Land whereon is Smith's shop being part of 10 acres which I bought of Capt:n Gwyn Reade.

I give my Son Jaquelin the remaining 9 acres ... and also the one acre after my son John's decease.

I give my son John and to his Heirs for ever all my Lands in James Town Island which I purchased of Christopher Perkins also the Ferry house and the Land belonging to it out of the Rent of said Ferry he shall pay my Son Jaquelin 20 pounds yearly during the space of 10 years from the time of my death. I give my said son John and to his Heirs for ever a small piece of Land near his house which I purchased of Mr. Edw'd Travis who bought the same of Mr. Drummond it formerly belonging to John Harris to whom Mr. Sherwood sold it being part of 3½ acres which the said Sherwood bought of John Page Esq.

I give my said Son John and his Heirs for ever my Plantation on Powhatan Swamp, which I purchased from his Aunt Mrs. Martha Jaquelin, I also give him the Negro Slaves imployed thereon ...

(End of p. 1 of the Ms.; it contains a signature of Rd. Ambler.)

I give my said Son John Three Leases of 310 acres of Land scituated in the Maine near James Town which I held of the Gov'r. at the yearly rent of 62 bushels of corn.

I give my son John all my Negroe Slaves which are employed at James Town Island and the Maine ...

I give my said Son John all the House furniture left in my House at James (one word scratched out or worn away) together with the Dairy woman named Moll Cook, Negroe, Hannah Jaquelin Phillips boy Cupid The three Carpenters Vizt. Old Ben Mark and John

I give my son Jaquelin 1000 pounds sterling in the hands of Mess'rs. Edward Athawy and Company of London.

I give my Son Jaquelin and to his Heirs for ever my Lot of Land and the Houses erected thereon scituated between Fort Hill and Churchyard now in the tenure of John Gibbons.

I give my son Jaquelin and to his heirs for ever one acre of Land which joines to York Town part of the acre is a garden on the other part are houses in the occupation of John Davis.

I give my son Jaquelin two Negroe boys now on black Swamp Plantation named Ned and George also two boys at York Town named George and Guy and Old Edith's two girls named Grace and Venis Also my Negro Woman named Grace which is now sick.

I give my son Edward all the furniture of my dwelling house he acquitting my promise of the House and Lot now in the tenure of John Gibbons which by this Will I give my son Jacquelin but if Son Edward insists on my said promise then I give my Son Jaquelin all the furniture of my said house, that is to say, my plate bedding Tables Chairs and all Utensils belonging to my dwelling house kitcheon and

Stable.
My stock in trade ... due from my son Edward and John and the amount of all I give my Son Edward and my Son Jaquelin to be equally divided between them and it is my request they carry on Trade in Partnership. I give all my Bonds and Obligations which are not Entered in my Storebook to my said Sons Edward and Jaquelin to be equally divided between them.
(End of p. 2; signed Rd. Ambler.)
I give my Son John and to his Heirs for ever Two acres of Land in James Town Island bounded to the South by the River to the North by the Main road to the East by a small Marsh which divides it from the ferry house Land which two Acres was given me by Mr. Edw'd Jaquelin's Will. Note I have given Mr. Johb Smith and my son Edward by Deed their Live in the two acres.
I give my Son Edward my Slaves undermentioned, to wit Old Edith Peg Abel Will America Sawney Polly Jerry Genney and Carpenter named Sharper and his son named Ben.
I give my grandsons Edward and John two boys named Ned and - (worn). Also I give them Little Edith and Peg's boy named Billy.
I give my grand daughters Sally & Molly youngest child named Hannah (daughter of Peg) and Polly's childed named Tamo.
It is my desire that Martha Gooseby be paid out of my store goods 20 pounds in consideration of her care in attening my dear daughter in her last sickness if Mrs. Gooseby die then the 20 pounds to be paid to her children.
... Lastly I appoint my three sons Edward John and Jaquelin Ambler Executors ...
(No wit., no date, no proving, no Rec.)   Signed Richard Ambler.

Ms. # 124.

Indenture, 4 May 1767, Between William Holt of the City of Williamsburg of the one part & Edward Ambler Esq. of the Town of York of the other part. Witnesseth that for And in Consideration of the said Edward joining in a Bond with the said William as his Surety to Francis Jerdom of Louisa Co., 2000 pounds Cur. Money ... the said William Holt as a Counter Surity to the said Edward Ambler ... sold ... Land in James City Co., whereon the said William hath lately erected a Merchant (?) Mill, 115 Acres, also 1500 acres of Land part in the said Co. of Jas. City and part in the Co. of Chas. City which he bought of John Son Marston & Richard Graves near the sd. Williams Forge. Also half that Tract of Land on which the said Forge is erected ... with the Forge Saw Mill and Grismill.

Wit.: Will. Sanghorne   Signed & sealed;   William Holt
       Will: Goosley   covered by strips   E. Ambler.
       Cary Goosley   of paper for protection.

On the other side: At a Gen'l Court at the Capitol, 21 Oct. 1767, ordered to be recorded.

Ms. # 125.

Indenture, 9 May 1767, Between William Warburton of the Co. of Sussex & Allisand his wife of the one part & Edward Ambler of the Co. of York Merchant of the other, for 60 pounds Cur. Money ... sold ... unto the said Edward Ambler ... Land lying and being in the Parish of James City, 120 acres, bounded as followeth, to wit., Beginning on James River at a corner Pine (as before).

Wit.: Edward Wilkinson   Signed: William Warburton.
       William Gibbs
       Robert Higginson

On the Other side: Court, Jas. City Co., 11 May 1767, ordered to be recorded. Test. Ben: Waller Cl Cur.

Ms. # 126.

Indenture, 18 May 1767, Between Jaquelin Ambler of York Town, Merchant & Rebecca his wife of the one part & Edward Ambler of the afore said Town of the other, for 50 pounds of Cur. Money ... sold ... unto Edward Ambler ... all that Lot or half acre of Land lying in the

Town of York aforesaid bounded as follows on the North East side by a Lot belonging to & now in the possession of Mrs. Hannah Mills, on the South East Side by the Street running from the River Southerly & on the South West by another Street cutting the Former at right angles & on the North West by the land of the said Jaquelin Ambler.
No   Signed with two seals; covered with   J. Ambler
Wit.   strips of paper for protection.   Rebecca Ambler
    Court for York Co., 18 May 1767, ordered to be recorded.
      Test. Thos. Everard Cl Cur.

Ms. # 127.

Indenture, 18 May 1767, Between Jaquelin Ambler & Edward Ambler (as before) ... half acre of Land, Town of York, known & prescribed in the plot of the said Town the Figures 34 which said Lot or half an acre of Land was devised by the last Will & Testament of Richard Ambler ... unto his son the aforesaid Jaquelin Ambler ... unto the said Edward Ambler
No   Signed and with 2 seals   J. Ambler
Wit.   probably.   Rebecca Ambler.
    Court for York Co., 18 May 1767, ordered to be recorded.
      Test. Thos. Everard Cl Cur.

Ms. # 128.

Sir   Westham   April 15, 1773.
Letter concerning a platt "which I drew soon after my return in March" ... Signed and probably once sealed. Saml. Jordan.

Ms. # 129.

Indenture, 27 Nov. 1779, Between Mary Ambler, of the County of Hanover, of the one part & Capt. Edward Travis of the City of Wmsburg of the other, for 5 Shillings ... granted and to Farm let ... unto the said Edward Plantation in James Town Island where the said Mary lately resided ... except a Nursery adjoining to the Mansion House which is to be reserved for the Use of the Ferry and the Ferry to the same belonging or in any wise appeartaining ... Rent of three Hogsheads of inspected Tobacco containing at least 3000 pounds.
Wit.:   Edm'd Randolph   Signed and probably   Mary Ambler
      Elizabeth Harrison   once sealed.   Edw'd Travis.
      Lewis Nicholas   (No recording.)

Ms. # 130.

      Henrico   Sir
John Ambler & Geo. Nicholas Enters (as in the Ms) with me for all the lands beginning at the Mouth of West Ham Creek on James River Thence on the Old lines of the land of the late Wm. Byrd Esq. dec'd. to the lands Late Ben: Clarks thence up the Back lines of the lands of R. C. Nicholas Estate & so on the Lands of Colo. Tho. Randolph & thence down James River to the beginning. Warrant for 6000 acres, certified by my hand & seal, 22 May 1783. No witnesses are given.
        Signed   Tho. Prosser   I. H. C.

Ms. # 131.

Indenture, 6 Nov. 1787, Between the President & Masters or Professors of the College of William and Mary in Virginia of the one part & John Ambler of the Co. of James City of the other part ... grant ... sell ... to the said John, Land in Jas. City Co., 367 acres, bounded, to wit, Beginning in the road at the corner between Ambler, Harris & Travis, the description under which this corner was lately known & running South ... to James River, thence down the River South ... to the ferry road; thence East 32 cha: to the creek; thence running up the Creek North ... following its meanders to Wilkinsons Land; thence leaving the Creek & running along Wilkinson's line South ... to the old field; thence West ... to the ferry road; & thence up the said road to the beginning: Land ... vested ... in William & Mary College in fee simple by an Act of Assembly, May 1784.

```
No            Signed and once       James Madison
Wit.          with large seals.     G. Wythe
                                    Robert Andrews
                                    Charles Bellini.
       Court, Jas. City Co., Ordered to be Recorded.
          Test. Ben: C: Waller C:C:
```

Ms. # 132.

Indenture, 19 Oct. 1809 Between Charles McGill, Alfred Powell & Robert Page, Commissioners appointed by the Superior Court of Chancery for Staunton District in and by a Queeree of the sd. Court rendered 28 March 1808 in a cause depending between George F. Norton complainant and Hugh Holmes and others the Representatives of John Hatley Norton dec'd. and others, defendants of the other part, and John Ambler of the City of Richmond ...

Ms. # 133.

In the Name of God Amen I Wm. Brisco of James City et a
Item i give & bequeath to my said daughter in Law Anne Holder, all my Land in James City adjoining Mr. Henry Hartwell, and that Land that was Mr. Thomas Rableys, now in ye tenure of Mr. Joseph Toping as marrying Elizabeth ye daughter of ye sd. Rabley, being a quarter of an acrea ... I purchased of Mr. Thomas Holyday ...
   Copia Vera   Test al p Clerk p MC: Cl Cur.

Ms. # 134.

   Platt: Mr. James Land. Land for Wm. Sherwood, 15 Aug. 1680,
20½ Signed Jn. Soane.

Ms. # 135.

   Plat: 119 Acres, 9 cha: 13 Dec. parts. Signed John Underhill.

```
    119 Acres, 99 Cha: 53 p:   (* The number 5 is written over,
     10         *52       00       illegible, ut addition is
      3          44       37       proof.)
    ___          40       00    Total sum of all Parcells
    133          35        9    surveyed for Mr. John Knowles,
                                 6 Aug. 1664, S:r Met.  JS
```

Ms. # 136.

Plat, no caption, no date.

Ms. # 137

   Platt. On back: Col. Swan's figure in James City Island, 37½ Acres.

Ms. # 138.

   Plat. On back: A Sketch of Webbs Pat. sent to me by Mr. Duval.

Ms. # 139.

Part of Webb's Platt to Mr. Nicholas. Sent to me by Mr. Duval.

Ms. # 140.

A Platt drawn by Collo: Jordan after he had been upon the Survey.

Ms. # 141.

   Platt. No caption, but Tuckaho is in the description & also Tuckahoe Island Creek. On the back: figures are visible in a computation, but the back has been pasted over it. Also on the front side:

John Ferrars 176 Acres.   320 / 1175 / 3   In Square in the middle:
                                 960   3256 Acres.
                                 ───
                                 215

The End.

Instructions, Etc., 1606-1683, Ms. Vol., Virginia, pp. 169-177.
Several grants, Patents, belonging to Sir Wm. Berkeley.

p. 169.

William Berkeley sells to Coll. Edward Hill Esq., one of the Council of State, 500 Acres, bounding East, on Alestres and Mr. Chiles lease, West on the great creek, South on Mr. Drummonds lease, and the river, North on Sir William Berkeleys land, 27 March 1661.
Signed Wm: Berkeley
Recorded 15 April 1661.   Tho Brereton, Cl. Con. Exam. & Rec., 6 Oct. 1668.

I Collo. Edw:d Hill Esq., acknowledge the sale, 28 March 1661.
Wit.: Tho. Ludwell   Signed Edward Hill.
      M. Hammond
      March 28, 1661   Ack. in Court, 15 April 1661, Tho. Brereton, Cl. Con.

p. 170.

ffrancis Morrison, Esq., Gov'r., grant ... farme lett unto Sr: William Berkeley, 8½ acres of land in Pasbehay s, near the Blockhouse, bounded, vizt. North West upon a ditch devideing this land from ye land of Mrs. Perkins, South East towards the Blockhouse, South West towards the River, and upon the River, and North East upon a swampe dividing this land from the land of Mr. Coleman, 1 August 1662.
Signed   Francis Morrison.
Test: Fran: Kirkman. Exam. & Rec.: Test: Hen: Randolph Cl Assem.

Francis Morrison to Sir William Berkeley, 5,062 Acres, scituate in James Cittie Countie, lying betwixt the heads of Poetan Swamp & Jones Creek, bounded, vizt., from an Ash tree standing in a little swampe, from thence North 900 po: thence East 900 po: thence South 900 po: and thence West 900 po: where it began. The sd. land being granted to Sir William Berkeley by Patent 25 Mar. 1658 & now renewed by order of the Quarter Court, 27 Oct. 1662. Signed Francis Morrison.
Tho: Ludwell, Sec. Exam. & Rec., 6 Oct. 1668.   Test: Hen: Randolph, Cl. Ass'y.

pp. 171-2

5 June ... to board of Survey, by James Cocket & John Senior, Surveyors, lands belonging to place of Governor, 3000 acres, as 1090 acres belonging to Sir William Berkeley, for transportation of 22 psons, bounded North upon the land of Robert Wetherall, and William Edwards, East upon Poetan, South S:th East upon the land belonging to the place of Gov'r: West towards the land of Capt. Freeman & West upon Chichahominy path, which said lands by error of Survey as formerly made thereof, was granted by order of Court, 4 June 1643, being by that Survey the Quantitie of 984 acres, but upon a second Survey found to be 1090 acres, are now granted to Berkeley; 70 Acres by lease for 21 years, bounded North North West upon the same & South S:th East upon part of the said land belonging to the place of Gov'r. East North East upon Powetan & West South West upon James River.
Signatures: Jno. West, Rich: Kempe, Sam:ll Mathews, William Brocas, Tho: Pettus, Hen: Browne, Hump: Higginson, & Rich: Townsend. Vera Copia: Test: Fra: Kirkman Cl Con. 6 June 1646. Exam. & Rec.
Test Tho: Ludwell Sec.

pp. 173-4 Continued.

Confirmation of Preceeding & names of signatures given in the text, - Sept. 1664. Signatures: John Carter, Robert Smith, Tho: Stegg, Hen: Corbyn, Tho: Ludwell, Tho: Swan, Nath: Bacon & Ab: Wood. Rec. in Sec's Off at James Cittie. Fra. Kirkman.

p. 174.

Names of those transported, 1090 Acres, 6 June 1646.

Rich Selden	Rich Welberry	Alice Vynall
Tho: Bristow	Eliz: Alesbury	Mary Trason
John Williams	Tho: Bassett	John Cole
Robert Wincoff	Will: Lamb	Rich: Purdey
Robert Haines	Jane Strahell	Roger Lynns
Tho Yeales	Robt: Buxton	John Gilly
Will: Jaceson	John Allingsworth	Bryan Bushton
Robert Jones	Nich: Danber or Dauber	Edw'd. Higby
Jo:n Ashbyfoot	Tho: Etherall	Geo: Hughs
Wm. ffowles	Tho: Mason	Leo: Partich
John Dance	Tho: Mallard	Rich: Swan

Exam. & Rec., 6 Oct. 1668.

p. 175.

Richard Bennet ... grant ... to Sir William Berkeley 1090 acres (bounds are given as above) ... due by transportation of 22 psons, 6 June 1646, and Rec. 9 Oct. 1652. Signed: Richard Bennett, W:m Claiborno, Secr: Exam. & Rec., 6 Oct. 1668. Test: Hen. Randolph Cl. Assem.

Francis Morrison ... grant to Wm. Berkeley, 2090 Acres, James City Co., bounded, Vizt.: 1090 acres (as before) & 700 acres another part, West upon the land of Thomas Stone and part of the land of Rich'd. Bell South into a branch of Powhatan Swamp for bredth runing East Northly up the side of Poetan Swampe one mile and 3/4 and East up into the woods 320 po: for length by the side of William Stevens, and 300 acres the residue hereof lyeing upon the head of the land of Rich:d Bell, runing North

p. 176.

and South upon the head of Bells land for length 150 po: South upon land of Xian Williams and John Edwards, and East by North up into the woods, 320 po: up by the said Williams & Edwards land. The said land being due to Wm. Berkeley as followeth: 1090 acres commonly known by the name of Green Spring by a Patent dated 9 Oct. 1652, and the other 1000 by purchase from Robert Wetherell who assigned this Patent, dated 20 May 1648 unto the said Sr. Wm. Berkeley, 17 March 1661. Signed Francis Morrison, Tho Ludwell, Sec. Rec.: Fran: Kirkman Cl. Con. Exam. & Rec., 6 Oct. 1668. Test: Hen: Randolph.

Francis Morris lease to Sr. Wm. Berkeley, 120 Acres, lying in the Mayne, known by the name of Racefield, bounding, vizt.: South & South West on Mrs. Perkins land, South East on ye Marsh East on Causyes land, North on a Pocason & West on the Maine River, 1 August 1662. Signed: Francis Morrison. Test: Francis Kirkman, Cl. Con. Exam. & Rec., 6 Oct. 1668, Hen: Randolph.

p. 177.

1 June 1643, Present: Sr. W: Berkeley, Capt. Jno. West, Mr: Rich: Kemp, Capt. Wm. Pierce, Capt. Brocas, Capt. Pettus, Capt. Bernard, Mr: Ludlow & Mr. Stegg. To Berkeley, 984 acres, adjoining the land successively belonging to the Gov'r. & Commonly known by the name of Green Spring, James City Co., bounded Vizt.: South South East upon the Gov'rs land, East North East towards Powhatan Swamp, North by West upon the land of Thomas Pall, South West by West upon the land of Mr. Grace & South upon Chicahominy path ... transportation of

underwritten persons (not given).. Vera Copia, Test Francis Kirkman, Exam & Rec. Test: Hen Randolph Cl Assem.

The end of this selection.

Foreign Business & Inquisitions, 1665-1676, Ms., i Vol.
Inquisitions for James City County

p. 54.

Patent, James City Co., 16 May 1638 to Benjamin Darrell, 700 Acres, found to escheat, jury 27 March 1663; Julian Allam, Widd., Patent to her, 7 Sept. 1665 & Rec. 16 Dec. 1667.

p. 68.

James City Co. Inquisition, 20 Dec. 1666, before Miles Cary, 11 Dec. 1666, etc., John Turner, at the time of his death, was seized of a pcel of land of 30 or 40 acres in M'chants hundred parrish in James City Co., formerly purchased of Richard Barnhouse; John Turner left 2 sons behind him, John & George Turner, which are since dead in thier minority; sd. John Turner made no will & there is no heir. Jury (all with seals)

Edw. Ramsey	Thos. Twade	Jno. Hayman
And. R. Reador	Fran. Wyth	Robt. R. Shoar
Wm. Whittaker	Wm I Paulett	Jno. Littler
David Crafford	Clemt. Haydon	John F. Cole

p. 156.

James City Co., Inquisition, 27 of 7ber 1670. Patent, 25 of 7ber 1668, Granted to Thomas Swann & concerning land to Tho. Ludwell. Disputed by Thomas. Jury (all with seals):

Isaac Watson	Walter Chiles	Rich. Holden
Tho. Hunt	Wm. Susnett	Wm. Mayes
Tho. T. Cogin	Rich. James	James Alsop
Wm. Stanton	Wm. Wrugy	George Marable

p. 228.

James City Co., Inquisition, 2 Dec. 1675. Granted to Peter Varny Lands Jno. Grubury had at the time of his death and by his petition in right of his wife & Escheat John Dobonias & by Thomas Woringtons Petition to the same in Wilmington Parish & John Dobonias was a ffrenchman and therefore an alien & the land to Escheat, 160 Acres. James Bray deputy Escheator & the Jury: (all with seals) (Note: difficult to read.)

Tho. Young	Tho. Bridges	Will. Brown
Rich. Beardwell	Alex. Walker	Nich: Bush
John Deane	Tho. Milton	Jos. Bush
	Jo: Merryman	

Other side of the Book, p. 15.

By Patent dated at James Citty, 16 May 1638, 700 Acres to Benjamin Carrell, Dec'd. & for want of lawful heirs escheated & by Jury 27 March 1663 & to Julian Allam, Widow, 25 Dec. 1665 & Rec. of Wm. White, 19 June 1667.

The End of the Inquisitions for James City County

The Land Patents For James City County.

Book 6:

p. 39.

To all & Whereas & Now know yee that I ye said Sr. Will. Berkeley, etc., give and grant unto Emannell Cambew negro 50 acres of Land according to the ancient Lawful bounds thereof, scituate in James Citty County, the said Land being part of a Greater Quantity formerly granted unto Will Davis and Lately found to Escheate, 18 April 1667.

p. 42.

Mr. William May, 100 Acres of Marish Land Lying and being in James Citty County below Goose hill bounded vizt. Northerly on the Land formerly Maj. Hobbs now in possession of Jno. Barber, Northerly on Jno. Pimhorne, North East on Parchmores Creek, South East on the Main Riv., South West and South East on Will Sarsnett & South West on the Maine Riv. the said Land being formerly granted unto Thomas Woodhouse, and Wm. Hooker by Patent dated 21 July 1657 and by them deserted ... granted by the Gov'r. and Council ... 15 April 1667.
    Charles Greene   Wm. Landers

p. 90.

David Crafford, 86 acres, 29 cha: & 6 Dec. pts of land in the parish of Martyns hundred in James City County, beginning at a corner stake on the South side of Church path in Mr. Richard Whittacres lyne thence East South East 3/4 East'rly 9 cha: 4 primes to the Church pathe and near the Dead mans stake, thence along the said path severall courses ... thence along Wm. Bedfords lyne North by East 98 cha: to a corner sweet gum nere the run at Greenes Swamp thence up the same ... thence by Mr. Whittacres lyne ... to the place where it began. This said Land being part of a patt:t of 1500 acres formerly granted unto Mr. Tho: Loveing Dec'd. by patt. Dated the 14th of Oct. 1643 and since became due unto Mrs. Anne Loveing as heir of the said Thomas, and since purchased by the said David Crafford of the aforesaid Mrs. Anne. 7 Aug. 1667.

p. 153.

Mr. Richard Whittacre, 135 acres, 66 cha: James City Co., 120 acres, 66 cha: bounded as follows as beginning at a corner poplar in a branch of Greene swamp by Capt. Ramsyes corne field from thence by the old lyne of trees ... to a bottom and run, thence down the same courses 60 cha: the poynt next the River thence 7 cha: to the point of marsh next the house thence up the marsh side on all courses ... to a forked branch thence up the west'rmost part thereof ... thence up the said branch ... to a corner hiccory marked three ways nere the head of the said bottome thence ... to a corner poplar on the south side at Green Swamp thence up the same ... to the place where it began. The residue being 15 acres of Marish land lying between James river the bounds at Mr. Tho. Loveings land and the aforesd. Devdt., the said Land being due unto the said Whittacre as followeth, 100 acres part thereof being given unto the said Whittacre by Maj:r Wm. Whittaker his Dec'd. father & 40 acres the residue by & for the Transportation of one person. 28 Oct. 1666. Peter Johnson

Book 6, p. 169.

Thomas Maples & William Hitchman, 200 Acres, James Citty County, and on the branches of Warrany Creek, beginning at a marked white oake on the burchon Swamp and standing in Sr. John Aytons lyne thence ... along the Swamp side to a marked red oake thence North West 194 po: to a marked tree in the horse path to a marked tree ... thence ... to a marked tree on the Tymber Swamp side thence ... to a marked tree in Sr. John Aytons lyne thence ... to Sr. John Aytons corner tree thence ... to the place where it first began. The said land due by

transporation of 4 persons, 10 Sept. 1668.
Trage Okey, Rice James, Anne Jones, ffrancis chandler.

p. 170.

Thomas Maples & Wm. Hichman, 536 acres, James Citty Co., and on the branches of Warrany Creek, beginning at a marked Spanish oake on the Tymber Swamp side and adjoineing to the land of Wm. Elcome thence East up the said Swamp according to the several courses thereof 185 po: to a corner stooping marked white oake standing nere Mr. Sorrells path then ... to a corner marked oake on a branch of Warrony Swamp thence ... to a marked tree neare an Indian field, thence ... to a corner marked pokecory standing on Warrany maine Swamp thence ... to a corner marked birch tree belonging to Mr. Burnetts land and standing in Sr. John Aytons lyne thence along the said lyne ... to a corner tree of the said Aytons land thence ... to a corner tree in Wm. Elsomes lyn thence ... to the place it began. Due by transporation of 11 psons, 10 of 7ber 1668.

Tho. Grymes	Hump: Clarke	Edw: Allosser
Geo: Bayley	Gerard Green	Wm. Payne
ffra: Oatby	Jno. Light	Charles fforbody
Anne Barber	Mary Watts	

p. 201.

Mr. Edward Sanderson Merchant, 3500 acres, lying in James Citty Co., 2715 acres of the said land Surveyed by and of the Gen. Court, 25 Sept. 1664, by Maj:r Tho: Ligon on the East side of Chiccahominy river, North on Sandersons Creeke South upon the gutt or little Creek which parts the land of John ffelgate & Coll. Robert Holts from Sandersons as aforesaid and soe from the head of the same gutt or little creeke East alongst the marke trees beginning at a red oake at the head of a valley and from thence along the said lyne of marke trees crossing the path that goes from the sd. Coll. Holts to the said Sandersons still continueing the said East course to the lyne of trees which parted the land of Phillip Chesley, and the said Holt, but since the sd. Sanderson by purchase to the Maine branch of Cherkurus Creek and so along the said branch Northward untill you come to Sr. Wm. Berkeleyes lyne of marke trees which crosses the said branch of Checkurns, and Ridge from the hot water swampe, between the said Sr. Wm. Berkeley and the said Sanderson, and soe it continues and runs that course almost to the head of the said Sandersons Creeke to a great poplar marked with two chopps, and so West upon poyny point Creek and Sandersons Creek which is opposite and agt. the Islands of the said Sandersons and the River of Chiccahominy as afore specified. 26 May 1668... Surveyed by Mr. Rich. Lawrence presid:t to Coll: Edmond Scarburgh Surveys Gent. for the said Sanderson three Islands lying in the said County of James Citty and on the East side of the Chiccahominy River, called by the name of Hope Island al Morgan Island, Great Island and Little Island, the said Hope Island conteyning 107 acres and the Great Island 239 acres and the little Island 89 acres and the whole amounting to 435. Bounded Westerly upon Chiccahominy Maine River aforesd. So:ly upon pyney point Creeke, w:ch divides these Islands from the land of Coll. Robert Holt, Ely upon Sandersons mayne land included in the same patt. with these Islands and No:ly on Sandersons Creek w:th:in which bounds are also included severall small Islands conteyning all the firme and some sunken marsh intermixed adjoyning to the said Islands of woodland ground w:ch by estimation amounts (it being too troublesome to Survey being for the most part Impassable) to 350 acres, part of 3000 acres, 24 of 7 ber 1665: by Maj. Tho: Ligon's Survey it amounts to 3715 acres with the maine land & this contains 435 acres & the woodlands of the Islands & the sunken Marsh contain 785 acres & rights for 500 acres bounded East upon Sir Wm. Berkeleys lyne and the Maine branch of Checkurus, North on Sandersons Creek, South upon the gutt w:ch parts the land of Jno. ffelgate, and Coll. Robert Holt from Sandersons, and West upon the Chickahominy. The said land due unto Mr. Edward Sanderson as followeth: 3200 acres part of those formerly granted unto the sd. Sanderson by patt. dated 20 Jan. 1650, and ... purchased of Phill. Chesley by the sd. Sanderson, and

200 acres another part since being due for transporation of four psons, and that Island that was formerly Mr. Wm. Morgans, aforesd. was afterwards purchased by one John Browning of the sd. Morgan, and sold by the sd. Browning to one James Cockett and the sd. Sanderson by Extent seized upon it as his right from the sd. Cockett for debt being 150 acres and since the sd. Sanderson added another right to it w:ch made 200 acres and due for transportation of one pson, and 500 acres more since, due for transportation, including in all 3500 acres, the quantity before expressed let it be more or less w:ch in the aforesd. bounds, dated 7 Oct. 1668.

Tho. Webber	Eliz. Blackley	Edward ffeilones
Owen Evans	Jno. Allen	Robert Allen
John Carpenter	Alex. Bugden	Kath. Hudson
	Wemih(?) Bedford	

p. 208.

Mihill Gowree, 30 or 40 acres, scituate in Mchants hundred parrish in James Citty Co., formerly belonging to John Turner Dec'd. and by him purchased of Capt. Rich. Barnehouse and lately found to escheat, and by a Jury for sd. County under hand and seale of Coll. Miles Carey, 20 Dec. 1666, & now granted to sd. Gowree, 8 Feb. 1668.

p. 214.

Thomas Swann Esq., 500 acres, James Citty Co., on the North side of James River being part of a devid:t of Mr. Rice Hoe next above Thomas Scotts Leased land sold by the said Hoe to James Warradine, South West on the River, East on the woods the said land being purchased by Capt. Edward Hill of James Warradine and by the said Warradine purchased of Rice Hoe and as due unto the said Tho. Swann Esq. by purchase from the said Capt. Hill. Dated 18 Dec. 1668. (Note: The index has 18 Sept. 1668, but December is plain in the test.)

p. 223.

Thomas Ludwell and Thomas Stegg, Esq:rs, half an acre in James City on the River side and adjoining to the westermost of those three houses all w:ch Joyntly were formerly called by the name of the old State house, bounded, vizt., beginning at the South side of the said house West to the wall where the said Westermost house joyns to the middle house, thence running South Westerly 34 deg., 67 feet, to high water mark, thence ... up the river side. ... thence ... through the said Old State house and the partition wall dividing the sd. Westermost house, and middle house 114 ft. & ½ to the place where it first began the said course being Correspondent and agreeable to the Azimuthes of the four side walls of the house and making quantity aforesaid. The said land being due by and for building a house in James Citty aforesaid. 1 Jan. 1667.

p. 246.

Francis Sanders, 130 acres, James Citty Co., and at the head of a Creeke issueing out of Chickahominy River called Jones Creeke bounded as foll. vizt: beginning at a mked great poplar standing on the South side of the swamp at the head of the said Creeke a little above the mill and running from thence ... thence West along the swampside 93 po: to the place where it first began including the quanity aforesd. 100 acres pt. thereof being formerly sold by the Hon:ble Sr. Wm. Berkeley unto Wm. Dubosse and by him assigned unto Mr. Edward Gunnell and by the sd. Gunnell assigned unto the sd. Mr. Francis Sanders, and 300 acres for transportation of 1 pson, 17 June 1669.
Hen. Musson

p. 298.

Mr. Mathew Paggs, 1250 acres, James Citty Co., in and adjoyning to neck of land being bounded by Back River & its marsh on the one side unto a marke white oake by Mr. Batts his landing thence by a marke post runing North East ½ North to another marke white oake on the maine branch of Gleab Land Neck which said Land & Neck with its marsh and swamp bounds the residue of the said Land also 250 acres of Marsh land be it more or less being all the marsh between the high Land & Creed making it a neck (Vizt.) Gleab Land Creek & back creek opposite to the first survey and grant for the said neck of Land and the annexed devident the said land being in all 1500 acres the marsh included the said land being formerly granted to John Crump by patten(t) dated 29 Nov. 1654 and by the said Crumps will given to be equally divided between his wife Elizabeth & his Daughter Elizabeth which said Daughter dieing by the said will was given to the survivor & therefore was due to the said Elizabeth late the wife of John Crump aofresaid & now the wife of the said Mathew Pagg and was freely given by the said Elizabeth to the said husband Mathew Pagg, by deed in Court 2 Dec. 1657. Patent, 19 March 1662.

p. 389.

Mr. Wm. Drummond, 1442 acres & 1 Rood, in Chickahominy River, James City Co., vizt. 1200 acres part of reof? being formerly granted unto him by Pattent 26 March 1662, beginning at ye next point of Land above Warrany Landing place, lying West Southerly upon ye said Chickahominy River & East Northerly upon ye main woode, Warrany Creek on ye Northerly side extending East Southerly down to Warrany Landing place for ye breadth with marsh and swamp adjoyning to ye said quantity of acres, the said land being formerly graunted to William Taylour by Pattent, 9 Nov. 1638, and 242 acres on Rood other of the said 1442 acres, 1 Rood, formerly granted by pattent to Edward Cowles & Phillip Charles, 6 Aug. 1666 and by them assigned over to ye said Drummond, 29 Sept. 1668 being a Neck lying in Chickahominy River on ye North side of James Citty bounding as follows beginning over against a clay point of Gregory Wells his Land next towards Ould feild and running Northwest 112 po: South East, & on South West by South ... & said land being due to ye said Cowles & Charles by & for transportation of 5 persons, --- 167-.

p. 389.

I Sr. William Berkeley ... for the better strengthening of James Citty It was ordered by Act of Court bearing date 14 June 1638 that ye Mayne Land in Pasbehayes on this side of Powhetan Swamp should be leased out ... term of 21 years deferring to the Governor and his Successors the Annuel Rent of Two Bushells of Indian Corn for every 50 acres ... Mr. William Drummond, 200 acres, James Citty Co., in Passbehayes, vizt. West North West upon the Land of William Drewit (? or Drecoit) North by West upon the land of Mr. John White, East by North on ye land of Daniel Liell South by East upon the Land of Sr. ffrancis Wyat, and South West by West upon the River, from the feast of St. Michaell the Archangell last past, annual rent of eight barrells of merchantable Indian corn shelled, to be paid at ye dwelling house of the said Mr. Drummond scituated upon the land aforesaid, payment to begin 29 Sept. next ... dated --- 167-.
Memo. in the Margin: that these words (according to an Act of Court dated 25 Nov. 1671) were enterlined before the sealing of this lease.

p. 403.

John Bowman, 108 acres, 3 Roods, on the North side of James River in James Citty Co., and on the west side of Chicahominy river adjoyning to Thomas Tinsley lying & bounding as followeth vizt. beginning upon a Path called Ridge Path & running along the path West by North 148 po: to a small speckled oake West South West 234 po: to a great white oak in a ffork of Moses Run North East half East 300 po: to the place aforementioned and is due to John Bowman for transportation of 3 persons, 15 May 1673 Anno 24 Car. 2d Regis.
Bryan Rooke   Wm. Taylour   Anthony Johnson

p. 413   (No County Index)

(Walter Chiles pcell of Land lying and being in James Citty Island called and known by the name of black Poynt East 30 cha: East North East 112 cha: to the River, thence along the River South 20 cha: and South South North 30 cha: to a marsh thence along the West 83 cha: and North North West 22 cha: to the place it began including 70 acres, which land was formerly granted to Walter Chiles father of the said Walter Chiles and by right of descending unto him as Sonne and heyr of his said father dec'd. 20 May 1670. A:o 22 Ca:r 2d.)

p. 442.

Rich: Holder, 8 acres one Rood & r Po: of Land scituate lying and being in James Citty and bounded as followeth, Beginning at a stake standing at High water Mark on James River side at the mouth of a Small Run Entering thereunto thence running North Easterly ... & thence South Easterly 36 deg: 18 po: to a persimon tree neere the corner of the orchard thence South Easterly ... thence South Westerly 70 deg: 25 po: to a stake on the Banke neare James River side thence North Westerly 36 deg: 38 po: along the River side to the place where it first begun The said Land being granted unto Rich Holder by an order of the Gen:ll Court held at James Citty, 12 Oct. 1670, and due unto him for the transporation of 1 person, 28 Jan. 1672. (the name is not given.)

p. 452

John Duke, 486 acres of Land, James Citty Co., upon the East side of Chickahominy River Butting North West upon Tyasoun Swamp Beginning at a white oake of a Devidend formerly belonging to Wm. Dormer Runing Downe the said Swamp 104 po: to 3 white oake trees A(?t the) corner of David Nowells Land & bounding along the Land of ye said Nowell South 65 gra: West 448 po: to a Redd oake In Robert Huberts line and by the said line South 49 gra: East 14 po: to a corner Hickory or a Oake nere the head of a valley and South ... to a branch and up the said Branch to a corner Gum in the Head of it North ,.. to the said Dormers Land and by the Land North 41 gra: West to Tyasoun where it first began. Due for transportation of 10 psons. 13 May 1673.

Phill White	Tho. Wright	Jno. Amory
John Haley	Wm. Bell	John Pacamon
John Wilkison	Nich. Baldwin	John Vordale
	Marj. More	

p. 495.

Mr. William Drummond, 461 acres, 1 rood & 4 po: of Land on ye North side of James River in James Citty Co. lying between the Orphant of Edloe his Land on the River and 700 acres belonging to the orphant purchased of Young on the head Lying and bounding as followeth beginning on the Round about Swamp where the corner of the Miles End standeth parting the orphant of Math: Edloe and the Land of Capt. Hubert ffarrell and runing from thence North East 240 po: to the Hoggyon Neck Gutt, then along the Gutt to Barker his House ... down Jno. Edloe his head line 340 po: to the place aforementioned. Due by (transportation) of 10 persons.   19 Oct. 1674.

Robt. ffarrar	Jno. Allen	Jno. Gammon
Jno. Crisam	Wm. Michell	Lawrence Cowch
Wm: Hearne	Susan Cutts	Susan Chiles
	Geo. Row Mingol Negroe	

p. 504.   (No County Index)

(John Duke, 136 acres of Land, in Chichahominy upon Tiaskun Swamp, beginning at Mr. Jos. Wadds Corner Gum & extending from thence North ... bounded upon Edw:d Gyllies Land ... down a Miry branch ... to a corner hickory by Tiasoun Swamp in the mouth of the small branch or slash ... to the Land where the said John Duke now lives ... to the place whereit began. Due for transportation of 3 psons. 15 Dec 1673.

Edward Griffith   Jno. Glanlin   Robt. Turtle
   (Note: this patent may not be in James City Co., but compare it
to the one of James City Co. to John Duke, Bk. 6, p. 452, this page.)

p. 519.

   Phillip ffreeman, 650 acres, James Citty County upon the Maine
Swamp of Chickahominy River above Westham Path and adjoyning to the
Land of Tho: Meredith and bounding as followeth: Beginning at Tho:
Meredith upper corner tree by Chickahominy Maine Swamp being a beach
running thence East North East to his corner oake North of the head
of a branch thence North along the line of Tho: London ... to the
Maine Swamp aofresaid and down the said Swamp to the place it first
began. The said Land formerly granted to the said Phillip Freeman by
Pattent 2 May 1661. Now dated 10 March 1673/4.

p. 521 (No County Index)

   (Mr. Robert Holden, 186 acres of High Land and Marsh Inter-
mingled & 64 acres of Marsh Land, 250 acres, Lying in Martins Hundred
parish bounded as followeth vizt., beginning at a Point Where Skiffes
Creeke and on Haymans Creeke joynes thence upp haymans Creeke to a
Branch thereof called Preand Dam Gutt Spring at the head of a branch
thence Downe the Said branch to Skiffes Creeke to the place where it
first began. The High Land being 150 acres purchased of Mr. ffra:
Kirkman and 100 acres the Residue newly take up & due by transportation of 2 psons. 21 Sept. 1674.
           Himself with Math Crosse.)
   (Note: this land may not be in James City Co., but the names
of the people in the patent have had residence there.)

p. 586.

   Theo. Hone Junr. & Tho: Hone, 736 acres, James Citty Co. & bounded
as followeth vizt. 200 acres pt. of the aforesaid Land beginning on
the branches of Warranty Creeke & at a M'rked white oake on the
Burthen Swamp & standing in Sr. Jno. Aytons Lyne then ... along the
Swamp Side ... to a marked Red Oake then ... to a M'rked tree in the
Horse Path thence ... to a m'rked tree on the Timber Swamp side thence
... along the Swamp side to a m'rked tree in Sr. Jno. Aytons corner
tree thence North East by East 84 po: to Sr. Jno. Aytons corner tree
thence ... to the place where it first began & bounded on the 2
distances by Sr. Jno. Aytons Lands, including the quantity aforesaid,
as alsoe 536 acres the Residue of the said Land on the Branches of
Warrany Creek beginning at a marked Spanish oake on the Timber Swamp
side and adjoyning to the Land of Wm. Elsom thence East by ye sd.
Swamp according to the several courses thereof 185 po: to a corner
stooping m'rked white Oake standing neere Mr. Sorrells pathe thence ...
to a corner marked oake on the ranch of Warrany Swamp thence ... to
a m'rked tree neere an Indian feild thence ... to a corner marked
pokeckory standing on Warrany Swamp Thence ... to a corner marked
Burch tree belonging to Mr. Burnells Land & standing in Sr. Jno.
Aytons Line thence along the said Line ... to a corner tree in Wm.
Elsoms line thence ... to the place where it first began ... Formerly
granted to Tho: Maples & Wm. Hitchman by 2 pattents dated 10 Sept.
1668 and by them is Lapsed for want of seating and since granted to
Jno. Wright by Order of Gen:11 Court 12 April 1674 and by him
assigned to Theo. Hone & Thomas Hone & is due by the transportation of
15 psons. 5 Oct. 1675.
Jno. Eallon   Marg: Lewis   Sarah Burdett
Wm. Moyle   (Note: only 4 names are given.)

p. 620.

   George Woodward, 200 acres, upon Tyascum Swamp, James Citty Co.,
pish of Wimbleton, bounded vizt., South East upon William Elcones
Land South West & West upon Tyasam Swampe ... unto the woods bounded
by m'ked trees on all stations as by the platt it does & may appeare
which said Lands being granted or assigned to the said George Woodward

his heires and assignes for ever by Sr. John Ayton, as by Pattent, 15 Oct. 1653, will appear. Undated.

p. 690.

Mr. Henry Hartwell, 736 acres, James Citty Co., and bounded as followeth (Vizt.) 200 acres pte. of the aforesaid land beginning on the branches of Warrany Creeke and at a marked white oake on the Burthen Swampe and standing in Sr. John Aytons line thence ... along the swamp side to a marked red oak thence ... to a marked tree on the timber Swampe side thence ... to a marked tree in Sr. John Aytons line ... to the place where it first began and bounded on these two differences by Sr. John Aytons lands including the quantity aforesaid as alsoe 536 acres the residue of the said Lands on the branches of Warrany Creeke beginning at a marked Spanish oake on the timber Swamp & side and adjoyning to the land of William Elcombe thence ... to a stooping white oake standing neare Mr. Sorrells path thence ... to a corner marked tree neare an Indian feild thence ... to a corner marked pochickory standing on Warremy Maine Swamp thence ... to a corner marked burch tree belonging to Mr. Burnell land and standing in Sr. John Aytons line thence ... to a corner tree in William Elconbes line then ... to the place where it first began including the quantity aforesaid ... Formerly granted to Thomas Maples and William Hitchcock by two pattents, 10 Sept. 1668 and by them lapsed for want of seating and since granted to John Wright by order of the General Court whoe assigned the same to Theophilus and Thomas Hone whoe pattented the same but not "pforme the same according to the pvison" in the pattent and by order of the Gen:ll Court in April last the said land was granted to the abovesaid Henry Hartwell. Transportation of 15 psons (the names not given). 30 May 1679.

Bk. 7, p. - (No County Index)

(Isaac Coates, 418 acres, on North side of James River on ye South side of ye run of Moses Creek bounded as foll., from ye Runn into y woods along by Moses Marked trees to ye aforesd. Moses Corner tree ... thence ... along Mr. Bishops marked trees ... down to Moses Runn thence down the runn as ye Runn winds to ye place where it began. The said land was formerly granted to Barth Knipe by pattent, 6 Oct. 1652 & for want of seating or planting by him deserted & the land granted sd. Coates by ye Gen:ll Councill, 15 Instant; for transportation of 9 psons; 30 April 1680.
The Index has 21 April 1680.

Tho: Moor	Jno. Hoskins	Tho. Sadler
James Mason	Jorie(?) Miles	Sara Morris
Arthur Mandy	Peter Long	Henry Mayden)

(Not in James City Co. Index. p. 22. (Not in No County Index.)

Dame Frances Berkeley, 285 acres, James City Co., bounded Viz., from a white oake at ye head of ye Long Meadow South ... on Wetheralls old Line to Coll. Holts Land & thence 77 cha: North to a white oak on her Lady:ps devidend of Land called ye hot waters thence running East upon ye old Line ... to a Leaning Hickory and thence South ... to ye place which began as by exact plott thereof may more plainly appear. Due by transportation of 6 psons. 20 April 1680.) (The persons not named.)

p. 22.

William Soanes, 420 acres, James Citty Co., on ye North side of Chickahominy River beginning below ye mouth of a Slash of Tyesun Swamp thence runing West by South half a point Southerly 65 cha: on Dormers Old Line thence ... thence ... to Mr. Wades Land along w:th his & Edw. Gilles downe against to Tyescun Swamp of sd. Land being ye bounds on ye other side being part of a pattent of 450 acres formerly taken up and assigned to ye sd. Wm. Soanes. Due by transportation of 8 psons.
20 April 1680.

Tho: North	Anne Poor	Jone Vahan
Edward Huck	Geo. Morse	Robt. Davies
Mary Swann	Law. Bromfeild	

p. 25.

William Whittacre, 400 acres, part in James Citty Co. & part in York Co., bounded as followeth, Vizt. beginning at a m'rked white oake standing at ye forke of a swamp near Wm. Pauletts Lands & bounded East with Tho. Bucks Land on ye North with Mr. Robt. Harris Land on ye West with Mrs. Higginsons Land & on ye South West with Coll. Tho. pettus his Land including ye quantity aforesd. Due by transportation of 8 psons.
20 April 1680.

| Wm. Whittacar twice | 3 negroes | Jno. Congers |
| | Eliz. Langley | |

p. 43.

Garrett Johnson, 1140 acres, James Citty Co., on the North side of the head of Chickahominy River and is bounded as followeth (Vizt.) beginning at a gum on the upper side of Barbadoes runn and runing North ... to the edge of Chickahominy river Swamp and so through the swamp to the river and downe it to the mouth of Barbadoes run & by the same againe to the first mentioned gum the said devident of Land being formerly graunted to the said Garrett Johnson by Pattent --- (the space is in the Ms.).
Due for transportation of 20 psons.   10 July 1680.
    (Note at the foot of the record.) The Records have been exactly Searched for ye date of ye originall pattent but by ye miscarriage of some part of ye Records in ye late troubles many matters are missing of which this can(n)ot be found.
    Nicho. Spencer Sec:ry   Recorded p. Hen. Hartwell Clk. The only names under the patent: Wm. Branin, Nich. Pryor, Ja: Varney.

p. 44.

Thomas Warberton, James Citty Co., 430 acres, bounded as followeth (Vizt.) beginning at the Mouth of a small slash issuing out of Pagan Creeke Swamp and thence along a line of old marke trees ... to a Spanish oake ... to a Saplin by a small meadow side and then ... to a round oake in the first mentioned line (including 40 acres of land which the said Warbarton purchased of John Knight dec'd) and a long the said line ... to the forked branch and up it to the great forked poplar at the head thereof and thence North ... to the head of Long Neck Swamp and downe the same to the mouth of Pagan Creeke and up the said Creeke to the place it begann. Being formerly graunted and now surveyed Exactly bounded, 10 July 1680.

p. 95.

Thomas Bobby, 500 acres, wanting 3, on the West side of Chickahominy river, James Citty Co., bounded as followeth (Vizt.) South South West upon the land of Humphry England North West upon the land of Thomas Wardon and East upon the river the said land being formerly graunted unto William ffry by Pattent dated 29 Aug. 1643 and by Lydia Noell and Elizabeth Jones by deed duely executed to the said Thomas Bobby; 23 April 1681.

p. 95.

Nicholas Bush, 317 acres, James Citty Co., on the North side of James river and on the East side of Chickahominy river beginning at a marked tree on the West side of Jones his Swamp and along the head of the Swamp untill it meets with old Mr. Knights line thence West along his marked trees ... to the maine Swamp then ... to John Merrymans marked trees 80 cha: to the Swamp and along the said Jones his Swamp to the place wee gegann. The said land being formerly graunted to Nicholas Bush father of the said Nicholas Bush by Pattent, 6 April

1655; renewed in his Maj:ties name by order of the Quarter Cort, 21 Oct. 1662. Due the said Nicholas Bush as heir of his said ffather. 23 April 1681.

p. 96.

William Browne, 970 acres, James Citty Co., on the North side of Chickahominy river being commonly called and known by the name of ffort land formerly belonging to Mr. Thomas Rolfe dec'd. and is bounded as followeth beginning at a red oake on the river marsh at the mouth of Nanbepoy Neck and thence North ... along an old markt line to a gum in Nabepoy runn and up the said to a branch and up the said branch to a great poplar thence along a line ... to a hickory in the corner of William Webbs plantation thence North ... to Richard News corner oake thence North ... to the head of a branch of Rabennetts runn and down it to the forke thereof and up the other to thereof to an oake att the head thereof thence (to) Esq. Diggs line of old marked trees South ... to Webbs Spring branch and down it to Rabennetts runn to the River and downe the River to the place it begann. Due as follows, 525 acres pte. thereof being formerly graunted to Thomas Rolfe Gent. by Pattent, 8 Aug. 1653 and 300 acres other part thereof was likewise graunted to the said Thomas Rolfe by Pattent, 25 April 1656 and fifty acres other pte. thereof was graunted to the said Thomas Rolfe by Pattent, 16 Oct. 1658 and the other 95 acres residue thereof being within the bounds always accounted part of the said ffort land and is due to the said William Browne by and for transportation of two psons, 23 April 1681 (the persons not named.)

p. 97. (No County Index.)

(William Sherwood, 28½ acres, lying att the mouth of James Citty Island and is bounded as followeth (Vizt.) beginning at James River at the head of a great slash issuing into the back river and downe the said slash East ... to the back river marsh and up the same to a marked persimon tree under block house hill point thence under the said hill west 6 cha: to James River and downe it again to the first mentioned slash, including 8 acres and thence again & downe the said slash 40 cha: to Mr. Richard James land and along it South 23 cha: to a branch of pitch & Tarr Swamp thence up the said branch to James River and up the river to the place it begann, conteyning 20½ acres. Formerly granted to John Baldwyn by Pattent, 4 Oct. 1656, for 15 acres 59 po: more or less and now by a late Survey found to conteyne 28½. The said John Baldwyn by his last Will & Testament in writing did under his hand and seale give the said land to John ffulcher and his heirs for ever which said John ffulcher by deed under his hand and seale, 22 Oct. 1677, acknowledged and recorded in James Citty County Court sould conveyed the same to the said Mr. William Sherwood and his heires forever. 23 April 1681.)

p. 98.

Mr. William Sherwood, 1 acre, James Citty Co., on which formerly stood the brick house, formerly called the County house which said house and land formerly belonged to the County and by the Hono:ble The Grand Assembly was sould and assigned to Major Richard Webster and by the said Webster assigned to Richard Ricks Dec'd. and afterwards by order of the Hono:ble Governor and Councell, 17 Oct. 1660, was sould and assigned to John Phipps whoe sould and conveyed the same Deed under his hand and seale, 5 Oct. 1661, and recorded in James Citty Co. Court to John Knowles and his heirs which said John Knowles by deed under his hand and seale, 23 April 1667 acknowledged and recorded in the Gener:ll Court sould and conveyed the said house & acre of land amongst other lands to Jonathon Nowell & his heires for ever whoe dying w:thout issue the same descended and came to David Nowell brother and heire at law to the said Jonathon. And the said David by deed of Sale under his hand and seale, 1 ffeb. 1677, acknowledged and recorded in James Citty County Court sold said house and the said Acre of Land to the said William Sherwood and his heires for ever. And the said Mr. William Sherwood hath since now built a faire house and appurtenances on the same which said acre of land begins at a stake before Coll. Whites Dore thence running towards his house ... to the place it begann, 23 April 1681.

p. 109.

Samuel Pond, 290 Acres, James Citty Co., formerly granted to Margaret Pond als Morley and was found to escheat ... Matthew Kemp Escheator of the said County ... Jury ... 29 Sept. 1680 ... now granted to the said Samuel Pond, -- 1681.

p. 123.

William Peawde, 1000 acres, James Citty Co., on the South side of Chickahominy River bounded vizt. Beginning att a markt Beech in the mouth of Mattahancks Necke and over the said necke to Webbs Run and soe up the said Run to a markt oake neer the head of the main branch then ... to a markt hickory in Nicked Owans Path, so North ... soe downe North East along Coakins branch to the back of Mr. Hams line to a markt poplar on the head of Nickudewas Run and soe Northerly and Westerly down the said Run to a markt Pine on the Edge of Maskout and soe down the said Run to a markt gum upon the East side of a little creeke which includeth a small Indian Field in the bottom of Maskout, including in all 1000 acres, which said land was formerly granted by Pattent, 11 Feb. 1663, to the said Wm. Peawde and George Sanders, who held in joyntenancy and now due to the said Wm. Peawde in right of survivorship. 20 April 1682.

p. 174.

Mrs. Mary Wade, 463 acres, James City Co., upon a branch of Tiascun, which 463 acres of land, together iwht 100 acres more belonging to Joseph Preston, is bounded as followeth Viz., Beginning att Grimes Old line of markt trees and running North 50 deg: Eastly 35 cha: to Capt. Hen: Dukes corner Hickory and along his line ... thence ... to South Swamp against ye mouth of Prestons Spring branch and up ye sd. branch to a white oake at ye mouth of his spring slash and thence North ... to a corner hickory, standing by Esq. Brays plantation and thence along Mr. Burnells land South ... to a white oake on Warrany and down ye sd. Run to ye aofresaid Grimes line and along it South 40 deg: Eastly to ye place it began. The said land being formerly granted by Pattent, 8 March 1658, to Mr. Thomas Hampton for 400 acres and by hime (ye above mentioned 100 acres of Prestons only excepted) on 30 Nov. 1670 assigned to ye said Mary Wade, by ye name of Mary Duke and farther due by and for transportation of 4 psons. 20 April 1682.
Fra Heyne   Robert Griffith   Robt. Cannon
                    Morris Mosely

p. 181.

Thomas Bowry, 120 acres, James Citty Co., lying on ye South Side of Chickahominy River in ye ark of Arrapors Swamp, bounded vizt.: Beginning at Mr. Travis corner red oake on the head of Arropor Swamp at ye corner branch a nd running along ye sd. Travis old line of markt trees West ... thence ... to a gum at ye head of ye upper branch of Arropor Swamp and down ye sd. branch to ye first mentioned branch and up yt to ye place it first began, which sd. Land is due unto him ye said Thomas Bowry by transportation of 3 psons. 22 Sept. 1682.
Wm. Hawly   John Wilby   (No more.)

p. 183.

John Hicks, 183 acres, James Citty Co., Bounded as followeth. Beginning at an oake standing on ye South side of ye South Swamp over against ye mouth of Prestons Spring branch and running South ... to Capt. Dukes upper corner oake and along his land South ... to a corner white oake, standing neere ye quarter Swamp, thence along ye land belonging to ye orphans of Mr. Collins dec'd. North ... to a gum

49

standing on the South Swamp, neer ye head thereof, and down ye said Swamp to ye first mentioned oake. The sd. land being due by transportation of 4 psons.
22 day of 7ber, 1682 (the index has 22 Oct. 1682.)

Hen: Roberts   Fra: Dawes   Jo:n Smith
Ralph Bassel

p. 203.

Ralph Burton, James City Co., on ye North side of Chickahominy river, containing 200 acres, beginning att small saplins in Mr. Dancies head line and along ye same North ... to a splin in black Swamp and down ye sd. Swamp to a Spanish oake in Thomas Timslies line, and along ye same South ... to an oake att ye mouth of ye sd. Swamp on Moses run, thence down ye sd. run to a black pine and thence North ... to ye place it began. The sd. land being due to ye sd. Burton his purchase from John Williams (as appears by bill of sale) Son and heir of Richard Williams dec'd., to whom ye sd. land (being part of 755 acres) was granted by Pattent, 3 Feb. 1651. Rec. 20 Nov. 1682.

p. 221.

John Dean, Jas. City. Co., part also in New Kent, 285 acres, bounded vizt., beginning att Doughts Spring & runing ... to an oake by Rickahack path & over it ... to an oake thence along Crooked Irregular line of old Meshed trees ... to Farthings Spring and down it to Arrow Reed Swamp & up the Swamp to a corner white oake & thence South ... to the head of a spring & down to a white oake corner tree thence South to the head of a Branch & down it & on one fork to the next & up that Branch to a corner gum thence... to Doughts Spring Branch & up it 4 cha: to the head thereof the sd. Land being purchased of Jno. Smith & Jno. Williamson for 350 acres & according to the most ancient & apparant bounds now Surveyed. 22 Dec. 1682.

p. 222.

Charles Goss, 275 acres, Jas. City Co., lyeing on the North side of Moses Creek to begin at ye Lower side of Kerbies Creek a little above the mouth thereof and runs North ... to Henry Youngs corner oake & thence along his & Thomas Bobbys marked trees ... thence South 39 d. Westly 163 cha: to a small Spling on Moses Creek & down ye same to Kerbies Creeks mouth & over ye same to the place it began the land formerly belonging to Eddy Goss & since was found to Escheat ... Inquisition ... hand & seales of Henry Hartwell Deputy Escheator of the sd. County, 7 June 1681.
Granted to Charles Goss, 22 of xber 1682.

p. 228.

Mr. Edward Travis, Jas. City. Co., 550 acres, bounded as followeth, beginning on James River att Black Point & runing up the river to the mouth of Pasmores Creek & up it to Cockett Neck Fork & up the Westermost Branch thereof to the head & thence to the mouth of the next Northermost Branch of the Marsh of the sd. Creek & up the sd. Branch to the head thence by marked trees ... to a pine on pitch & Tarr Swamp and down it to a marked oake on the upper side of the next Branch Issuing out of the sd. Swamp thence ... to Back River & down the same from the head of Harmans Creek to the place it began Including also within the sd. bounds 12 acres of Land belonging to Mr. Holliday w:ch Dividend of Land is due to the sd. Travis viz: 326 acres by Pattent, 10 Feb. 1663 relating to a second pattent, 10 March 1653. 150 acres by purchase from Jno. Seimer, 5th of 9ber 1654. 12 acres by purchase from Jno. Crump, 4th of 10ber 1654, and 15 acres purchased of John Johnson, 8th of Aug. 1659. 70 acres by purchase from Mrs. Susanna Chiles, 7 Aug. 1672. And 12 acres from Wm. Champion, 15 Nov. 1677. Rec. 22 Dec. 1682.

Bk. 7, p. 244.

Thomas Walter, 400 acres, Jas. City Co., Bounded (Vizt.) begining att an old corner white oake, standing 2 cha: off of Poplar Spring branch & runing South ... to Hitchocks line of marked trees, and along it North ... to an oak saplin in Masons line and along it North ... to a branch of Webbs Swamp & down it to the said Swamp & down the same to the mouth of Poplar Spring branch & up it as far as the first mentioned white oake, the said land being due by and for the transportation of 8 psons.
16 April 1683.

Jo: Reynolds	Timothy Pell	Wm. Hardin
Tho: Anbehl	Robt: Dale	Wm. Clerke
Law: Baker	Robt: Titterbon	

p. 251.

Mrs. Lydia Nowell, 357 acres, Jas. City Co., on the North side of James River Bounded Vizt. from a corner oake of Mr. John Edloes standing on the West side of Wolfes Plantation South West 169 cha: sown to James River, and up the same to Ellibris line of marked trees, and along it North ... to his corner white oake and thence North ... to the first tree, Including the Plantation called Foremans, the said land being purchased, 27 Sept. 1655, of William Fry Gent. of Rice Hoe Gent. for 252 acres, the Residue being due by and for transportation of 3 psons.   16 April 1683.

Hen: Bowser   Sam: Eldridge   John Rosse

p. 264.

Edward Ellerby, 100 acres, Jas. City Co., & bounded as foll: (Vizt.) from James River along Mrs. Nowells line of marked trees North ... thence on her head line South ... thence ... to James River and down the same to the place it began. The said Land being part of a Pattent of 600 acres granted to Haveat, 20 Oct. 1661, who by his last Will & Testament, 26 Aug. 1663, did give and Bequeath the same to William Strong who on 8 Oct. 1675 by Deed under his hand ... conveyed ... 100 acres ... to Stephen Butts & is due to the sd. Ellerby by purchase from the said Butts by Deed, 17 Sept. 1677. Rec. 16 April 1683.

p. 265.

John Doby, 362 acres, Jas. City Co., bounding as foll:o (Vizt.) from James River along Edward Ellerbyes line of marked trees North ... to an oake on Drinkards line and down it South ... to a white oake standing in the head of a little Creeke at Mount Sinai Bridge, and down the said little Creek to ye River and down it to ye place we began. The said land being due to the said Doby as foll. Vizt. it being part of a Pattent of 600 acres granted to William Haveat, 20 Oct. 1661, who by his last Will & Testament, 26 Aug. 1663 ... bequeathed ... to William Strong, who 30 Jan. 1677 sold ... 100 acres part thereof to ye aforesd. John Doby, and by his last will bequeathed 50 acres more of the said Land to him the said Doby, and ye Residue being 212 acres he the said Strong did by his Will dated 28 Aug. 1675 give and Bequeath unto William and Hester Thomas, who on ye 1 Aug. 1676 assigned ... aforesd. John Doby, 16 April 1683. (Note: the dates of the wills in the years 1677, then 1675 are underscored in the text, so that the confusion may have been in the original.)

Bk. 7, p. 265

William Hunt, 675 acres, Jas. City Co., & bounded as foll. (Vizt.) beginning att a Red oake att ye head of Arroper Swamp alias ye head of ye lower branch thereof and runing South ... over Pease hill Creek to an oake thence South ... to an oake, standing neere Oaken Swamp, thence West 90 cha: to a stake in ye South sied of the Rige feild through the Oaken Swamp South ... thence South 72 cha: to an Oake on Pease hill Creeke, and down it to a Pine, thence North ... to a gum on ye aforesaid Branch of Arroper and up it to the first Red Oake, the said land being part of a Pattent of 1080 acres granted to Mr. Edward Travis, 27 ffeb. 1643, and by him deserted and since by order of the Gen:ll Court, 23 Nov. 1682, granted to the said William Hunt ... transportation of 14 psons.   16 April 1683.

Tho: Lund	Wm. Hills	Rich'd. Paine
Jo:n Cassick	Jo:n Watson	Lucy Stratton
Dam: Watnye	Robt. Parker	Maurice Smith
Judeth Beach	Ell: Pickett	Jo:n Hancock
Tho: Reene	Hen: Dunnham	

p. 292.

Mr. Edward Chilton, 2 acres & 17 cha: Jas. City Co., bounding Vizt.: from Col. Phillip Ludwells corner stake South 88 deg: partly along his Hon:rs line ... thence ... along an old ditch 12½ cha: down James river bank and along under ye said Hill to a stake neer ye brick fort and thence North ... to ye first stake: the said land being due ... transportation of 1 pson. 16 April 1683. The name of the person: Peter Gibson.

p. 300.

Nath: Bacon Esq., 3 3/8 acres, Jas. City Co., bounded as followeth, Beginning att ye Eastermost Corner of ye "siad" Lawrences old ditch on a branch of Pitch & Tarr Swamp, and running South ... Westerly 2½ cha: neere ye end of a little Riling (or Ridge of Earth) and over it North ... to ye West side of ye aforesaid Ditch, and sown it to ye aforesaid branch of Pitch & Tarr Swamp, and down the said branch and ditch to ye first corner, being part of a parcel of land formerly belonging to Richard Lawrence, who being guilty of high treason ag:t his Majesty, not daring to abide a legal tryal, fled for ye same, whereby all his goods, ... forfeited... assigned to ye said Natha. Bacon Esq. ... by Deed ... 29 May 1683.

p. 307.

Edward Hooker, or Hooper, 87 acres, Jas. City Co., bounded Vizt. beginning att an Hash (? - confusion caused by a correction) line tree of ye Hotwater land standing in a small swamp, and Runneth Down the said swamp to Mr. Sandersons Mill pond, and up it to ye mouth of Jones Swamp and over it to Brownes Poynt, and up the North side of ye said Jones Swamp againe to the Hottwater Line and along it South ... to ye first ash (clearly given). The said Land being to ye said Edward Hooper (Note: Hooker is in the margin clearly & in the Index also, by the text however Hooper is clear.) & for ye transportation of 2 psons. 20 Sept. 1683. Paul Kinsey & Jo:n Kinsey.

p. 328.   (The index has p. 324.)

Thomas Wilkinson, 554 acres, Jas. City Co., where he dwells, on the South side of Moses Creeke, conteyning 554 acres bounded (Vizt.) from a pine in the head of the Westermost branch of Ware gutt South ... to Tial_os corner oake and along his line North ... to a broken oake in Phillips line and along it North ... to a branch of the hawkes nest gutt and downe them to Moses Creeke & down the same to the mouth of ye Ware gutt and up it & the first mentioned branch to ye first pine pte. of the said Land being pcell of a devident formerly held by Griffin Prickinson (or ? Wilkinson). The other part being due to the said Thomas Wilkinson all which Land being due unto him for transportation of 11 psons.   20 Nov. 1683.

Wm. Butler	Robt. Rigby	Walter Brooks
Wm. Posse	Jo:n Allam	T_o: Mitchel
Jane Baxter	Robt. Marlin	Ben: Caryl
Eliz: Caryl	Hen: Caryl	

p. 350.

John Soane, 457 acres of land, bying and being by supposition in Jas. City and Charles City County, Bounded Northward by the land of Joseph ffry, Westward by a Runn called Dockmans Run, Southward by the land of John Hix South Eastward by ye land of Mr. Bromfield, Eastward by ye land of Jerry Ham, and Jerry Ham Run, w:ch said land was formerly granted by Pattent, 20 April 1667 unto Curtis Land (see Bk. 6, p. 208 for a Patent to Curtis Land, but not indexed under Jas. City Co.) and by him deserted, after granted by order of ye Gen:ll Court, 18 Nov. 1674, unto John Wright and Cornelius Loften and deserted for want of seating, and now granted unto the sd. John Soane by order of Gen:ll Court, 20 April 1683 ... transportation of 10 psons.

Wm. Taylor	Wm: Raynolds	Wm: Coyt
Tho: Wood	Geo: Griffin	Apel Gaskine
Roger Adderson	Tho: Wormenel (?)	Nicho: Williams
	Anthony Obey	

p. 360.

John Dormer, 350 acres, Jas. City Co., which Mary Burney als Dormer late of the aforesaid County Dyed Seized of, and was lately found to Escheat ... inquisition ... Hon:ble John Page Esq. Escheator for the sd. County ... 28 July 1683 ... Rec. 20 April 1684.

p. 361.

Peter Glenister, 546 acres, Jas. City Co., formerly granted to a Margaret Barrett late of the aforesd. County dec'd. and was lately found to Escheat ... inquisition ... hands & seales of Mr. Edward Chilton deputy Escheator for the sd. County ... 14 Aug. 1682 ... Rec. 20 April 1684.

p. 361.

Mr. Henry Gauler, 418 acres, on the North side of James River, on the South side of y Run of Moses Creeke in Jas. City Co., Bounded as foll: from the Run into the woods along the Moses marked corner tree, South ... to Mr. Biships marked trees, thence ... down to Moses Run, thence down the Run, as ye Run winds to ye place where it began. The said land being formerly granted to Isaac Coates by Patent, 20 April 1680, and by him deserted for want of due seating, ... granted to him (Gauler) ... Gen:ll Court, 20 Sept. 1683 ... transportation of 9 psons. 20 April 1684. (Continued next page.)

Hen: Snow	Nicho: Barnet	Ed. Bland
Matt: Brisse	Hercules Messenger	Tho: Sweet
Jo:n Bell	Wm. Higgenson	Rose Hill

p. 366.

Mr. Humpherey Browning, 192 acres, Jas. City Co., bounded Vizt. beginning att a saplin standing on the South side of Jones his Swamp in the little neck, & runing along a Line of old marked trees ye sd. Brownings lower bounds of ye Lands he purchased of Thomas Meekins South ... to an oake on ye North side of Corne Swamp & down by ye side thereof, to another swamp called also Jones Swamp and down by it to ye Mill pond, thence up ye first Jones Swamp to ye place it began. The sd. alnd being due to ye sd. Humpherey Browning ... transportation of 4 psons. 20 April 1684.
Wm. Goldsmith, Wm. Rice, Edw'd. Windet & Wm. Johnson.

p. 382.

Rice Griffin, 197 acres, Jas. City Co., bounded from two poplar saplins, standing on ye South side of Pease hill Creek Swamp, North 70 deg: Easterly 24 cha: to an oake in a slash by ye Ridge path, and up the sd. path to Tinseley line of marked trees ... to Alcock corner pine in the aforesd. path, and up it to a Line of Potters field land, and along it North ... to a saplin on Pease hill Swamp, and down it to

ye first place it began. The sd. Land being due ... transportation of
4 psons. 26 April 1684. (The persons are not named.)

p. 385.

James Stratles, 240 acres, Jas. City Co., beginning on the East
side of the Iron mine meadow on Wetheralls line and along it North ...
to an ash tree standing in a Slash (neare the mouth thereof) and down
the said slash to Powhatan Swampe and up it ... to a poplar standing
neare the mouth of a Slash and down the said Slash to long meadow runn
and up it to Sir William Berkeleyes line of hotwater land and along it
North ... againe to Iron mine Hill meadowe and downe it to the first
line. 200 acres of the said Land being formerly granted to the said
James Stratles by Pattent, 14 April 1659 and renewed ... by order of
the Quarter Court and also granted to him by Pattent, 10 Jan. 1661,
and the other 40 acres being due by transportation of 1 pson. 20
April 1684.   Jeremiah Mathewe

p. 388.

Mr. John Soanes, 710 acres, Jas. Co., on West side of Chickahominy River, bounded Vizt. from Thomas Walters corner white oake
standing neere Webbs running on ye upper side of poplar Spring branch
South ... to the head of a Small branch of Hogpen Meadow and down it
to ye sd. Meadows and down the same... to Pease hill Creek, and over it
South ... to ye ridge path, and down the sound to potters field (als
Mr. Hunts land) and along it North ... to an oake neere Pease hill
Creek, and over it North ... to Thomas Bosoryes Corner oake, and along
his land West ... to a white oake in ye fork of a small branch of
Webbs run and down it to ye sd. Run, and up it to ye mouth of poplar
Spring Run and up it to ye first oake. The sd. Land being due unto
ye sd. Mr. John Soane ... transportation of 14 psons. 21 Aprill 1684.
(The persons are not named.)

p. 393.

Augustine Cobham, Jas. City Co., in the upper side of pease hill
Creeke, 66 acres (the margin says 76 acres), Vizt., beginning at Pease
Hill and at a line of marked trees belonging to Potters feild devident
of land and along it North ... to Pease Hill Run and then by it to the
first mentioned line. The said Land being due ... transportation of
2 psons. 26 April 1684. (Record does not give the persons.)

p. 398.

Mr. James Haley, 593 acres, Jas. City Co., bounded as foll:
Vizt. 493 acres part thereof being at a great corner pine of Jones's
standing att ye lower end of long thickett and runing South ... to
Doby's line, and along it ... to a pine in Wolfe's line, and along it
... to Lewis corner oake & along his line ... to Phillips corner pine,
and along his line ... to ye first pine, and 100 acres yq Residue
beg(inn)ing att an oake standing by ye cow path & run, cross James
Town Road, along Mr. Phillips line South ... to Mr. ffreemans line &
along it North ... to ye oake by ye path. Ye said 493 acres ...
granted by Pattent, 25 March 1656 & Renewed 18 March 1672 to John Shell
for 300 acres. And ye other 100 acres part of a pattent of 300 acres
granted to Griffin Dickenson, 5 Jan. 1656 & by him sold ... unto ...
John Shell by Deed, 11 April 1656, w'ch sd. John Shell, 10 March 1675,
sold to Lawrence Ash, who, 6 April 1676, sold ... to James Haley ...
transportation of 4 psons ... under the Pattent 26 April 1684. (The
persons are not named.)

p. 399.

Godfrey Spruell, 348 acres, Jas. City Co., w:ch together with 100
acres belonging to Hester Jones is bounded as foll.: Vizt. beginning
att a corner oake, standing by ye sd. Spruells Plantation, and runing
North ... to Woods corner oake, and along his line North ... to a white
oake on long thicket, and down it to a great pine, thence South ... to

Dobies line, and along it North ... to ye first oake. Ye sd. Land being due by transportation of 7 psons. 21 Oct. 1684. (The persons are not given.)

p. 438.

Clement Haidon, 277 acres, by order of the Gen:ll Court, 24 April 1684, whereon he now dwells in Martins hundred in Jas. City Co., beginning at 2 white oake saplins in James River & runing along the lower bounds of Grises land South ... to a white oake on Skeffe Creek thence down the said Creeke to James River and up it to the place it began including all marshes adjoyning to the said Land. (Scratched out: The said Land being due by order for the transportation of ffower pers.,) 100 acres pte. thereof being formerly graunted to the said Clement Haidon by pattent, 26 Nov. 1663, and the other 177 acres ... transportation of 4 pers. 20 April 1685. (The persons not named.)

p. 445.

Isaac Vadin, land in the upper part of Jas. City Co., 300 acres bounded (Vizt.) from David Corner hickory on Tyascun Swamp by his line South ... to the East corner of Hopkins his feilde then South ... to Tyascun Swamp it being the bounds in the other side. The said 300 acres of Land being due to said Isaac Vadin as followeth (Vizt.) it being the halfe pte. of 600 acres by the said Isaac & John Vadin purchased of Robert Crawley, 1 Sept. 1679 who on 2 April 1672 purchased the same of John Dormer and William Thomas the said 600 acres being the middle most pte. of 1100 acres granted by patent, 5 June 1656 to William Dormer dec'd. and by his last Will and Testament, 7 Jan. 1659, bequeathed to John and Rebecca Dormer. 20 April 1685.

p. 462.

John Vodin, 300 acres, Jas. City Co., on the North side of Chickahominy river and bounding as followeth (Vizt.) begining at Esq. Diggs (als Prosans) corner Oake standing at the head of Brownes branch and running thence North ... to Rabenetts run and up it to the uppermost side of the mouth of Browns maine branch thence North ... to the East corner of Hopkins his feild thence South ... to an ash by his plantation in Browns upper branch & down the run thereof to the mouth of the first mentioned branch and up it to the first oake. The said 300 acres of Land being due to the said John Vodin as followeth (Vizt.) it being the half part of 600 acres by the said John & Isaac Vodin purchased of Robert Crawly, 1 Sept. 1679, who on the 2 April 1672 purchased the same of John Dormer and William Thomas the said 600 acres of Land being the middlemost pte. of 1100 acres granted by pattent, 5 June 1656, to William Dormer dec'd. and by his last will, 7 Jan. 1659, bequesthed to John & Rebecca Dormer. 20 April 1685.

p. 481.

John Turner, Jas. City Co., 134 acres in the Pyney Woods, bounded (Vizt.) from Chickahominy Gate along Mr. ffreemans land North ... to the ferry path & along it to an oake standing on the Northeast side thereof then North 19½ cha: to a gum in the head of Cross Crooke bottom then along Godians Land South ... then along Hintons (or Wintons) South 21 3/4 cha: to an oake standing in the forke of the ferry path & ffreemans als Chickahominy path and along the said path being the bounds also of George Harbies land to the place it began including Pyney point (?) Swamp the said Land being due ... transportation of 3 psons. 4 Nov. 1685.

John Turner   John Grinfeild   William Watson

p. 498.

Richard Bennett, 430 acres, Jas. City Co., on the East side of the Chickahominy River adjoyning on Pagan Creeke bounded (Vizt.) from a gum the head of Bottom of Crosse Creeke South ... to a corner Spanish oake by Winters North ... to Warbertons corner saplins and

and along his Lyne South ... to Pagan Creek Swamp and over the said Swamp and downe the Southerly side of the said Swamp and Creeke to the mouth of Crosse Creeke and up it to the first mentioned gum. 250 acres of the said land being formerly granted unto Thomas Young by Pattent, 5 Jan. 1658, and renewed in his Maj:ies name, 18 Mar. 1662, sold by the sd. Thomas Young unto Andrew Godian by deed, 6 June 1679, who dyed, found to Escheat, by Inquisition recorded by Col. John John Page Escheator Generall of Jas. City Co., 14 Oct. 1685, granted to Richard Bennett ... 27 April 1686.
John Elock   Thomas Griffin   David Lacy
                      Wm. Knowles

Bk. 7, p. 515.

Gilbert Chancy, Jas. City Co., 50 acres, on the West side of Chickahominy River, beginning att a hickory in Mr. Cowles line of marked trees and from it South ... to peashill Creek, and down it to ye sd. Cowles aofresaid line, and up it South 84½ deg: Westerly through one corner of Bassetts ffield to ye first mentioned Hickory. The said Land being due ... transportation of 1 pson. 27 April 1686. (Person is not named)

p. 515.

William Peawd, of Jas. City Co., 400 acres, in ye upper part of ye County on ye West side of Chickahominy River, Bounded from Capt. Dukes corner oake in Gwins line South ... to a poplar standing in a branch of Webbs Run, and down this branch to ye sd. Run, and up ye Run to Walton branch and up it to ye head, thence South ... to Walters corner oake in Womsleys Line, and along it North ... to a white oake on ye North east side of Nicketewances path, and along ye sd. path over Mason & Bradfords paths ... to a poplar in a Branch of Poroham (or Toroham) Run & down ye Branch to ye sd. Run, & up ye Run to Gwins corner white oake, and along his Line South ... to ye first mentioned tree, 150 acres of ye sd. Land being due to ey sd. Peawd by pattent, 11 Feb. 1663, for 1000 acres, & 250 acres of Residue being partly surplasage land within ye Bounds of ye sd. Pattent ... transportation of 5 psons ... 30 Oct. 1686. (No names are given.)

p. 516.

Mr. ffrancis Dancy of James City Co., 287 acres, on West side of Chickahominy River, bounded from a dead gum on ye North side of black Swamp North ... to Tinsleys corner gum by a Slash, and along his line South ... to Black Swamp and up ye same to ye first gum, ye sd. Land being due ... transportation of 6 psons ... 30 Oct. 1686. (No names are given.)

p. 594. (No Co. Index.)

(William Winston, 21 Oct. 1687, 266 acres of land on which he now dwells, being part of a Pattent g:ted to Mr. Moses Davis, w:ch together with a parcel of Land now purchased by the sd. Winston of Mr. David Crafford.)

p. 597.

John Soane, a Triangular Devident of Land in Jas. City Co., on ye upper side of Pease hill Creeke, 66 acres, bounded Vizt. begining at Pease hill run at a line of markt trees belong to Potters field Devident of land & along it North ... to Pease hill Run, and up it to ye first mentioned line, w:ch sd. land was formerly granted to Augustine Cobham by pattent, 28 April 1684, and by him deserted for want of due seating, and now is granted to ye sd. Mr. John Soane by Or:r of ye Gen:ll Court, 27 April 1687 & due ... transportation of 2 psons. 21 Oct. 1687.   James Harris   Wm. Lendoll

p. 600. (No Co. Index)

(453 acres, 21 Oct. 1687, on North side of Jas. River, James Blair Clerke & the Easterly branch of the maine branch of Cornelius Run.)

p. 701.

Mr. Hen: Hartwell, 2 acres, 1 Rood, 24 po. & ½ of land (note: in the margin "½, nor index to Jas. City") Jas. City ... bounded as followeth, Beginning at a stake fixed in ye Bank of ye River, and thence by a line passing by ye angular poynt of ye branch, which faceth two of ye Eastern Bastions, of an old Ruined Turf fort, North ... where it hits on a line of ye land now or late of Mr. Sherwood thence along that line ... thence ... where it butts on ye Land now or late of holder ... thence by ye Land, now or late of Tho: Rabley, along ye Northern side of an old Ditch West ... thence along ye Western side of ye same Land late of Rabley South ... thence along ye Land, Late of James Alsop, ... thence along ye bank side of ye River up West ... where it began, half an acre of ye land by Pattent, 20 May 1661, granted to Mr. Wm. May; who by his will bequeathed ye same to Mr. Nicholas Merry weather, and by sd. Mr. Nicho: Merryweather by his deed of sale, 6 Feb. 1677, sold to Wm. White, who dying without heirs, sd. land was Lately found to Escheat ... Inquisition ... by John Page Esq. Escheator of ye sd. County... granted sd. Hen: Hartwell & one other half acre of ye sd. Land was by ye sd. Hartwell purchased of Coll. John Custis Ior Curtis) as by his deed of sale, 29 Sept. 1683, & Remaining part being waste land found adjoyning to ye sd. Land was granted sd. Hen: Hartwell by ord:r of ye Gen:ll Court, 8ber:26: 1688. Due by transportation of 1 pson. 20 April 1689. (The person is not named.)

Bk. 8, p. 42.

Mr. Wm. Edwards, 73½ acres, Jas. City & bounded from Joseph Copelands great gum on James River side a Long his Land North ... along ye Hon:ble Nathaniel Bacon Esq. his land ... to ye River and up ye same ... to ye aforesd. great gum being due unto ye sd. Mr. Wm. Edwards for Importation of 1 pson. 21 April 1690. The person: Jno. Roberts.

p. 43.

Elizabeth Marsten, 349 acres, Jas. City Co., formerly granted unto Wm. Wigg and by him sold and assigned unto Wm. Elcome by deed, 29 March 1657, and found to Escheat by Inquisition by Maj:r Sam. Weldon dep. Escheat:r for ye said County, 13 Oct. 1688, and is since granted unto John Marston, who hath bequeathed ye same by will duly proved unto ye aforesd Eliza. Marston, after having made composition, etc. Undated.

p. 53.

Mr. Jno. Soan, 82 acres, on West side of Chickahominy River in Jas. City Co., bounded from a corner white oake near Webbs Run along of bounds of his own Land South ... and to ye first white oake, North ... ye sd. Land being due unto ye sd. Jno. Soan by ye & for ye importation of 2 psons. 21 April 1690. The Psons.: Robert Smallpage & Jno. Ingerton.
(Note from the Index: See Bk. 10, p. 4, Henry Duke.)

p. 61.

Lydia Nowell Wido., 1752 acres, Jas. City Co., 750 acres, part thereof being formerly granted to one Wm. ffry and by Pattent, 17 April 1653, 252 acres thereof by one other Pattent, 6 Feb. 1655 & ye other 750 acres being also granted to ye sd. Wm. ffry by one other Pattent, 29 April 1656, which sd. severall pcells of land were also found to Escheat for want of heirs, of Joseph ffry, son & heir of ye sd. Wm. ffry as by an Inquisition, C. Wormley Esq. Escheator of the sd.

County, 10 July 1689, granted to sd. Lydia Nowell, 51 April 1690.

p. 64.

Jno. Wade, Jas. City Co., 34 acres, between Rockahock path Arrowreed path and Arrowreed branch bounded by them Vizt. North East on Roccahock path Southwest on Arrowreed path and Southeast on arrowreed branch ye sd. Land being due unto ye sd. Jno. Wade by and for importation of 1 pson. 21 April 1690. The pserson: Wm. Chessman.

p. 65.

Thomas Bobby, Jas. City Co., 750 acres, on ye West side of Chickahominy River, bounded as follow. Vizt., 500 acres part thereof South South East upon ye land formerly of Humphry England North West upon ye Land formerly of Thomas Warden East upon ye River and 250 acres ye Remainder, from a marked old tree by ye old cart way side North East by East 21 Cha: along ffrys Line North West 190 cha: thence to Richard Williams his corner tree, on a strait line West by South 95 cha: and th(en) along Richard Williams and David Phillips Lines, toye first beginning place, which Land for formerly granted to Wm. ffry by Pattent, 29 Aprill 1656; after his decease it descended to Joseph Fry, his Sone heir & he dying without will or heir, Escheated, granted by Patent to Lydia Nowell Wid., 15th of this instant April & she by deed recorded in the Gen:ll Court 29 of this instant April hath released and confirmed the same to Thomas Bobby, 23 April 1690.

p. 66.

Henry Soan of Jas. City Co., Gent., 1500 acres, in ye upper part of ye sd. County on ye West side of Chickahominy River, bounded as followeth Begining at a great dead corner pine Standing near Chickahominy River by ye mouth of a little neck or feild of Low Land called now by ye name of Walnutt feild, South ... to poplar branch & down ye sd. branch to Strawferry hill runth(en) down & over ye said run to a corner white oake on ye upper side thereof th(en) North ... to a corner oake of Williams Land, and along it North ... and partly along a corner of Strawberry hill run ... to two great old corner cypresses on Chickahominy River th(en) down ye sd. River to Wallnut field first mentioned and so about ye sd. feild or neck of Low Land - (including ye same) to ye first mentioned dead corner pine, ye sd. 1500 acres of Land being due unto ye sd. Henry Soan as follw. Vizt., 750 acres thereof by Pattent, 7 April 1653, to one William ffry, who died seized thereof, and after his Decease ye same descended to Joseph ffry Son & heir of ye sd. Wm. who died without will or heirs, land Escheated, & lately granted to Lydia Nowell Wid. by Pattent, 15 th of this Instand April, who by deed under her hand and seale, 19th this Instand April (acknowledged & recorded in Gen:ll Court) released assigned & confirmed the 750 acres to ye sd. Henry Soane, etc., & ye other 750 acres of land being due to said Henry Soan by and for ye transportation of 15 psons. 23 April 1690. (The record is continued on the next page.)

Tho. Parker	Andrew Broadhurst	Jno. Wheateby
Robert Leech	Sarah Roberts	Ambrose Edwards
James Turner	Tho: Shesard	Adam Holt
Wm. Jues (?)	Jno: Elsmore	Eliza: Janett
	Tom: Jack & Dick Negroes	(these may be two names)

p. 79.

Thomas Bobby of Jas. City Co., Planter, 750 Acres, on the West side of Chickahominy River, bounded as followeth Vizt., 500 acres pt. thereof South South East upon the land formerly of Humphry England, North West upon the land formerly of Thomas Warden, East upon the River, & 250 acres the Residue from a marked old tree by the old Cart way side, North East by East 21 cha: the nce along ffrys line North West by North 30 cha: thence to Rich'd Williams his corner tree on a straight line West by South 95 cha: & thence along Rich'd Williams,

58

Jno. Williams & David Phillips' line, to the first beginning place, which land was formerly granted to Wm. ffry his Pattent, 29 April 1656, after his decease itt came & descended to Joseph ffry his son & ehire, the same was lately found to Escheat, granted to Lydia Nowell Widdow the 15th of this Instand and April, & she by deed acknowledged & recorded in the Gen:11 Court, 19th of this Instant and April hath released & confirmed the same to the said Thomas Bobby, 23 April 1690. Note at foot of page: This Pattent & Record info: 65.

p. 81.

Tho: Charles of Jas. City Co., one island of Marsh, 115 acres, lying over Chickahominy River opposite to the Land he now dwells & is bounded South Westerly by the up(p)er Gulph of the sd. River & on all other sides by the River. The sd. Land being due unto the sd. Tho: Charles by & for ye Importation of 3 psons, 23 Oct. 1690.
Mr. Ellis Perry and Joanna Gon: Wm. Downes (the punctuation as of the ___)

p. 81.

Mr. Geo. Hunt of Jas. City Co., 200 acres, in the upper part of the sd. County, bounded Vizt., from Wm. Woods corner gum standing on the West side of Long thickett North ... to a corner white oake in Phillips Line & along it South ... to Halies Line & along the same South ... to a great corner Pine in the Drain of the sd. Long thickett (Including the same) to the first mentioned gum the sd. Land being due unto the sd. Geo. Hunt by & for the Imposition of 4 psons., 25 Oct. 1690.
Jno. Hubbert, Geo. Read, Gabriel Allen, Mary Taylor.

p. 82.

Jno. Howard, 172 perches of Land in James Citty, bounded from the North East of the Church yard a Long the Rayles the reof North ... to Hon:ble Nath: Bacon Esq. his Land and a Long it North 6 8/10 cha: to the corner thereof thence South ... to the old great Road and along the same to the first mentioned corner the sd. Land being due unto ye sd. Jno. Howard by and for Importation of 1 pson., undated. The Governor would not sign this patent of John Howard. The person named: Dan. Chesley.
Teste W. Edwards Cl Gen:11 Cor.

Bk. 8, p. 83.

Wm. Sherwood, Gent., 150 Acres, Jas. City Cty land, formerly granted to Rich'd James by Patent, 5 June 1657 and descended to Richard James his Sonn & was lately found to Escheat, Inquisition by Col. Ch. Wormeley Escheator of ye sd. County, 25 April 1689 & granted to ye sd. Wm. Sherwood, 3 Oct. 1690.

p. 108.

William Edwards, Gent., 736 acres, Jas. City Co., and bounded as foll. Vizt. beginning on ye branch of Warrary Creek, and at a marked white oake on ye Burehen Swamp, and standing in Sr. Jno. Aytons line th(en) North Westerly ... along ye swamp side to a marked red oake, th(en) North West 194 po: to a marked tree in ye horse path, th(en) North Westly ... along ye horse path to a marked tree standing by ye side thereof, then South Westly ... to a marked tree in ye timber Swamp side, th(en) South Westly ... along ye Swamp side to a marked tree in Sr. Jno. Aytons line, then North East by East 438 po. to ye place where it first began and bounded on these two Distances by Sr. Jno. Aytons land including ye quantity aforesd. as also 536 acres of residue of ye said land on ye branches of Warrany Creek - Beginning at a marked Spanish oake on ye timber Swamp side, and adjoining the land of William Elcomb, th(en) East up ye sd. Swamp, according to ye severall courses thereof 185 po: to a corner stooping marked white oake standing near McLowes path, th(en) North Westerly ... to a corner

marked oak, on a branch of Warany Swamp, th(en) North ... to a marked
three near an Indian feild, th(en) North Westerly ... to a corner
marked pockhiccory, standing on Warrany Maine Swamp, th(en) South
Westerly down ye Swamp 305 po: to a corner marked Burched tree,
belonging to Mr. Burwells land, and standing in Sr. Jno. Ayton's land,
th(en) along ye sd. Line South East ... to a corner tree of sd. Aytons
land, th(en) South West by West 58 po: to a corner tree in Wm. Elcombs
line, th(en) South along ye said Line 168 po: to ye place where it
first begann, whic sd. Land was formerly granted to Mr. Hen: Hartwell
by patent, 30 May 1679; and by him deserted, and after granted to
Edward Chilton by order of Gen:ll Court, 26 Nov. 1682, and by him
deserted and never patented, and is since granted to ye aofresd.
Wm. Edwards by order of Gen:ll Court, 18 April 1690; due for Importation of 16 psons, 3 Oct. 1690. The persons are not given.

p. 112.

Benjamin Eggleston, 595 acres, Jas. City Co., bounded as foll:
upon ye South side of Chicahominy River Beginning at a m:rked white oak
in Mr. Brumfeild line of M:rked trees, that standeth near a branch
that runeth into Chickahominy River, called ye great run where ffrancis
Storey now liveth th(en) West up ye sd. Branch to ye head thereof and
further to a m:rked white oak ... to a great pine that standeth by a
branch called Shaddocks branch, th(en) 100 po: th(en) down ye said
Branch bounding by it North West 80 po: th(en) bounding by ye sd.
branch ... to a corner white oak, that stands by ye said Shaddocks
branch, being a corner tree of a former divident of Land (land is
crossed out, but 2 "Of" s remain) of Mr. David Newels, th(en) South
East and by East, by a back line of ye said Divident of Mr. Newells
and so continuieing ye same course by a line of Mr. Brumfeilds land
to ye white oak where it first begann that standeth by ye aforesd.
great run 661 po: which said Land was formerly granted to Will Broadrib
by Patent, 6 Sept. 1665 and by him deserted and it since granted to
ye said Benj. Eggleston, 16 April 1690: and is due for importation of
12 psons.

Tho: Day	Wm: Horten	Brice Maybet
Edw:d Hinchin	Anth. Corbin	Brice Corbin
Tho: Coney	And. Yewren	Diana Jones
Jno. Lever	Nath. Newman	Anne Hupey

p. 123.

Capt. Hen: Duke, 1000 acres, Jas. City Co., on ye South side of
Chickahominy River, which was formerly ye land of Thomas Towner and
was lately found to Escheat, by Inquisition, Ch. Wormley Esq.
Escheator of ye said County, 24 Oct. 1689 & granted Capt. Hen: Duke,
23 Oct. 1690.

p. 146.

William Broadrib, Jas. City Co., 416 acres, in ye sd. County of
Powhatan Swamp, bounding from an old corner hickory (standing on ye
East side of the sd. Swamp where ye old Bridge was) South ... to a
stake in ye Hon:ble Xo; Wormeley Esq. his Line & along it North ... to
a small white oake standing at the - (scratched out) end of a wild
hedgrow, and along ye sd. hedgrow or Harrone (th eis confusion because
of scratching out) thickett (of partition of two feilds) to a Small
oak at ye other End thereof thence North ... to a white oake by ye
side of a branch of Drinking Swamp thence over the sd. Swamp North ...
again over ye sd. branch to an oake, thence North ... to an ash in a
branch, thence ... to a Gally (or Sally) on ye North side the sd.
Broadribs his Mill pond and down it to his Mill and down ye stream
thereof and ye run of Powhatan Swamp to ye first hickory which sd.
Land being due by and for ye transportation of 9 psons., 28 April 1691.
The persons are not named.)

p. 149.

William Bayly of Jas. City Co., 93 acres, bounded from an old

corner hickory standing on ye East side of Powhatan Swamp (where was
formerly a bridge) along Mr. Broadribs Land South ... to ye Roote of
a fallen hickory, South ... to a stake in ye Hon:ble Christ:r Wormeley
Esq. his line and along it South ... along ye sd. Esq. Wormeleys
Line to Powhatan Creek & up it so far as ye first mentioned hickory
Including all marshes, swamps and Sunken grounds. 50 acres of ye sd.
Land Hereditarily descending to ye sd. William Baily from his father
- (the space is in the Ms.) who purchased sd. Land of ye Rt. Hon:ble
Sr. Wm. Berkeley dec'd. and 43 acres ye residue being farther due, by
and for transportation of 1 pson., 28 April 1691. There is given the
person at the foot of the Patent: Eliz. Shepherd.

p. 167.

Mr. Mathew Huberd, 1500 acres, Jas. City Co., in upper part, on
ye North side of the head of Chickahominy River takeing in all that
can be at present found of a grater devident formerly granted by
patent to Mr..Robert Huberd Dec'd. for 2400 acres w:ch 1500 acres of
Land is bounded from Revenetts run or Mr. Marstons Line North... to an
oake by an old corner pine stump, South ... to Chickahominy River Swamp
and through it the same course 120 cha: to the River, and up the
River to ye upper Landing of Long Neck, and up the Uppermost Swamp
thereof to a great pine standing on ye Swamp above ye mouth of the
sd. neck, thence along Williams bound, North ... to a Slash, and down
it to Ravenetts Run, and over the run to a hickory, thence North ...
to an old corner stump, thence South ... to ye head of a branch of
Ravenett Run and down it and ye sd. Run to ye place it began. The
sd. 1500 acres of land being due to ye sd. Mathew Huberd as cozen
german and heir at law to Robert Huberd dec'd who was son and heir
of the above mentioned Robert Huberd unto whom ye sd. Patent of 2400
acres of Land was granted the 2 June 1651 (or 1657 or 1659; badly
scratched). 28 April 1691.

Bk. 8, p. 187.

Mr. William Hunt, 215 acres, Jas. City Co., bounded Vizt., from
a chesnutt Clake standing on the bank of James River somewhat below the
mouth of Little Creeke along John Clarkes Line North ... to a small
white oake, thence along woods Line South ... to a hickory, thence
along Ramballs Line South West ... to two pines on the River & up it
to the first mentioned oake the said 215 acres of Land being part of
a greater pcell purchased by Wm. Hunt (father of the aforesd.) of
Rice Hoe, 3:10ber:1656. 20 Oct. 1691.

p. 187.

Mr. Henry Randolph, Jas. City Co., 66 acres, on the upper side of
Pease Hill Run, at a Line of marked trees belonging to Potters feild
devident of Land, and a Long it North ... to Pease Hill Run, and up
it to the first mentioned Line. The said Land being formerly granted
to Mr. John Soane by Patent, 21 Oct. 1687, and by him deserted, and is
since granted to the said Mr. Henry Randolph by order of the Gen:ll
Court, 28, April 1691, and is due for Importation of 2 psons, 20 Oct.
1691.
James Varney   Robt. Clarke

p. 211.

Mr. Thomas Marston, Jas. City Co., 1300 acres, on the North side
of Chickahominy River, bounded from Chickahominy North ... to a pine
on the outward edge of the sd. River Swamp and thence ye same course ..
over above the fforke of Chessnutt Run ... to (Indian als) now
Invacon Swamp and down it to (Indian als) Barbadoe Swamp Run and down
it to Chickahominy River and down the same ot ye place it began. The
said Land being formerly granted to Richard Williams for 800 acres by
pattent, last Oct. 1653, and by him, 24 Jan. 1655, joyned to 750
acres more Lying on the upper side of the said River and being all
deserted this part was granted to ye sd. Thomas Marston by order of
the Gen:ll Court, dated James Citty, 15 April 1691, and is due for

transportation of 26 psons, 20:8ber:1691 (the index has 20 Oct. 1691.)

Math. Pyle	ffra. Peirce	James Polin
John Robinson	Robt. Redman	Jno. Smith
Rich'd. Smith	Ruth Symons	Sam:ll Thelfeild
Tho: Huby	Alex. Schofeild	Jno Goslin
Wm. Shilling	Rich. Jones	Tho. Waldrum
Edward Wright	James Welsh	Jno. Cutler
Toby Smith	James Turner	Andrew Coleby
Jno. Smith	Robt. Snead	

La: Nicholls (Puy Chambo Negroes.)   (Note: Punctuation of the Ms.)

p. 231

William Nance, Jas. City Co., 520 acres, on ye South side of Chickahominy River & bounded from a great corner pine standing on the West side a little Logie Slash next above ye plantation, whereon John Randall dwells, along Gregory Wells Land West ... to Ashes ffeild, and about ye South West side thereof (excluding ye field) to Mr. Bobbys Line, and along it South ... to a white oake on ye West side of ye Road and South ... to Lofftine corner pine thence along his Line North ... to a chesnutt oake on Chickahominy River Marsh thence along ye said marsh and river down & round ye sd. Nances (including of same) to ye mouth of ye first mentioned Lodgey Slash and up ye same to ye first-pine. 150 acres of ye said Land being due to ye said Nance by marrying -- (the space is in the Ms.) ye Daughter & one of the coheirs of Grace Tinsly who was Syster and one of ye coheirs of Richard Peirse Jr. being part of 600 acres granted to said Peirce by patent, 12 Sept. 1636 and 370 acres ye Residue due upon ye sd. Nances Survey of ye whole patent being found surplusage within ye bounds thereof it also due to ye said Nancy by & for ye Importation of 8 psons.
29 April 1692. The persons named below are given as they are listed.

Anne Keser	Wm. Kent	Eliz: Grocer
Nich. Prior	Wm., Kath Davis	Beirobe ffarmer

p. 232.

James Hood, Jas. City Co., 232 acres, from a white oake on ye East branch of Morgans Swamp, North 52 cha: to a white oak by ye sd. Hoods Horne thence North ... to a poplar on ye North branch of ye sd. Morgans Swamp, thence down & over ye said branch to a white oake on ye other side thereof, thence North ... to a small branch of ye sd. Morgans Swamp & down it to ye mouth of ye first menconed East branch & up ye Run thereof to ye place it began, ye Land being due unto ye sd. James Hood by & for ye Importation of 5 psons, 29 April 1692.

Robt. Bradly	Elizabeth Jennett	Nath. Tinberell
Hannah Bradly	Jno. Buberry	

p. 233.

James Barrett, Jas. City Co., Devident of Land called Peashill, 305 acres, bounded from a Spanish oake in ye East side of Peashill Creeke along Pruers Line of markt trees North ... to a pine on ye side of Chickahominy River Marsh and up ye side of ye said marsh and river to ye mouth of Peashill Creek and up ye East side of ye said Creeke & Swamp to ye place it began including all ye pine grounds and island slashes. The said Land being due to ye said James Barrett as son & heir of Capt. Wm. Barrett dec'd. ye former proprietor of ye said Peashill but by reason of destroing of ye Records the Title appears not therefore it is also further due by and for transportation (of) 7 psons, 29 April 1692.

Ellinor Keeney	Clement Loo	Jno. Hinich
Sibella Wood	Jno. Sorrell	Ann Blewet
	Prancer a Negro.	

p. 237.

John Stith, Jun:r, 595 acres, Jas. City Co., bounded as followeth upon the South side of Chickahominy River being at a marked white oake in Mr. Brumfeilds Line of Marked trees that standeth near a branch that runeth into Chickahominy River called the Great Run where ffrancis Story now Liveth, thence Westerly the said branch to the head thereof, and further to a marked white oake ... thence ... to a great pine that standeth by a Branch called Shaddock branch 300 po: thence down the said Branch bounding by it North North West ... to a corner white oake that stands by the said Shaddocks branch, being a corner tree of a former devident of Mr. David Newills, thence South East and by East by a Back line of the said Devident of Mr. Newells and so continuing the same course by a line of Mr. Brumfeilds Land to ye white oake where it first begun that standeth by the aforesaid great run 661 po. The said Land being first taken up by Mr. David Newill, 3 Sept. 1664, and by said Newill assigned and sett over unto the aforesaid (the first appearance of the name) Capt. Wm. Broadribb, 22 Aug. 1665, he the said Newill haveing never patented the said Land, and which Said 595 acres of Land was formerly (by patent, 6 Sept. 1665) granted unto the said Capt. Wm. Broadrib and by him deserted, and now again granted unto the said John Stith Jun:r by order of the Gen:ll Court, 8ber: 9:1691 and is due by and for the Importation of 12 psons, 29 April 1692.

Jno. Hair   Jno. Johnson   Guy, Will, Claye,
          Sue, Moriah, Hector, Pompy.   negroes.

p. 238.

Capt. Wm. Hunt, 610 acres, Jas. City Co., as followeth beginning at Moses Run at the mouth of a bryery Slash and up the said Slash and the Westerly branch thereof to a line of marked trees and along it East 98 cha: to a great pine thence along Travises Line North 80 cha: to a great pine in the North side of the Oaken Swamp and up the said Northermose side of the said Swamp to a white (als Long) Meadow and up the Eastermost side to an oake at the head thereof, thence North 27 cha: to Mr. Cowles head line & along it South ... to a learning white oake standing at ye head of Moses Run & down itt to the first menconed Slash. The said Land being purchased by ye sd. Hunt of Edmond Brewer by deed, 5 Dec. 1681, for 300 acres more or less according to ye said bounds. The said Land being due unto the said Capt. Wm. Hunt by & for Importation of 7 psons, 29 Aprill 1692.

John Green   Tho. Brown   Joseph Reuthan
John Arnold   Mary Woodbone   John Thomason
          John Coates or Catt (both are in the Ms.)

p. 253.

To all & whereas & now know ye that I ye sd. - (space in the Ms.) give and grant unto Mr. John Williams ... land ... 818 acres lying in Jas. City Co. on ye North East Side of Moses Creek bounded from an oake Saplin standing one ye side of ye sd. Creek Marsh a little above ye old Landing North ... to a Sally, & South ... again to Moses Creek & down ye same soe far as ye first mentioned oke Saplin. The said Land being due to ye sd. John Williams as son & heir of Rich'd Williams, dec'd. Vizt. 555 acres thereof being part of a Patent of 755 acres granted to ye sd. Rich'd Williams, 3 Feb. 1657. 100 acres other part thereof being part of 1330 acres assigned to ye sd. Rich'd. Williams by Wm. Strong, 7 April 1655 & 133 acres of residue being Surplus Land within ye said bounds is further due to him ye sd. John Williams. Importation of 3 psons., -- 1692 (blanks are in the Ms.). Margin: "Did not pass the Seal, not being any such County. R B Cl Sec Off:"

p. 276.

Thomas Bobby, Jas. City Co., 862 acres, whereon he now lives, bounded from Gregory Wells corner oake on Chickahominy River Marsh along the said Wells, Nances and Loftins Lands South ... to a white oake by the roade & South ... to Mr. John Williams Land and along his and Mr. Isaac Williams South ... to a small oake thence along Mr. Daveys Land North ... to a pear tree by Henshaws Plantation North ... to a branch of Beaver Dam Creeke & down it to Chickahominy river and up the said river and the side of the Marsh to the first mentioned oake. The said 862 acres of Land being due unto the Said Thomas Bobby Vizt. 750 acres thereof being granted him by Patent, 23 April 1691, and 12 acres the residue being surplus with in the Bounds of the aforesaid Patent, and is due unto the said Thomas Bobby by and for Importation of 3 psons, 29 April 1693.

Eliza Clark   Amy   Nero

Note at the foot: 750 & 12 are named in the Patent & 3 names under it. Not a good reckening.)

p. 300.

Stephen Cock of Henrico County a Devident of Land in James and Charles City County on the South West side of the head of Chicahominy river containing 1040 acres bounded from two old corner cyprusses on the said river below the Wadeing place South ... and partly along a corner of Strawberry Hill run ... Easterly through James Collaines cornfield 213 cha: to a hiccory on Chickahominy river and down the same to the first cypruss. The said Land being formerly granted to Richard Williams together with 800 more for 750 acres, by Patent, 24 Jan. 1655, and for want of seating granted to the said Stephen Cock by order of the Gen:ll Court, 17 Oct. 1690, being due unto the said Stephen Cock by and for the Importation of 21 psons, 29 April 1693.

Edward Elleston	Eliza. Skips	Rich'd. Brookes
Wm. Davies	Wm. Stephens	James Willis
John Soillman	four negroes	John Goram
Jane Tucker	Rachell Baker	John Seajam
Tho: Michaell	Roger Bolt	Hen: Richardson
Joseph Bucher	James Oglevy	John Butt

p. 315.

Philip Ludwell Esq., 1½ acres, adjoyning to the Ruins of his three Brick houses between the state house and County house in James Citty which land is bounded Vizt. begining neare Pitch & Tarr Swamp 8 cha: of the Eastermost end of the said houses and runing by the said End South ... thence North ... by the other End of the said houses and thence South ... to the place it begun. The said Land being due unto the said Philip Ludwell Esq. by and for the importation of 1 pson, 20 April 1694.

David Thompson

p. 320.

John Howard, 172 perches, James City, bounded from the North East corner of the Church yard along the Railes thereof North ... to the Hon:ble Nathaniel Bacon Esq. his land and along it North ... to the great old Road and along the same to the first mentioned corner the said Land being due unto the Said John Howard by and for the transportation of 1 pson., 20 April 1694. The Person: John Lever.

Bk. 8, p. 321.

Henry Duke, Gent., 736 acres, Jas. City Co., bounded as followeth Vizt. 200 acres part of the aforesaid Land begining on the branches of Warrony Creeke and at a marked white oake on the Birchin Swamp and standing in Sr. John Aytons line thence North Westerly ... to a marked tree in the horse path thence North Westerly ... to a marked tree on the timber Swamp Side thence South Westerly ... to a marked tree in Sr. John Aytons line, thence North East by East ... to the palce where it first began and bounded on these two distances by Sr. John Aytons land including the quantity aforesaid, as also 536 acres the residue of the said Land on the branches of Warrony Creeke beginning at a marked Spanish oake on the timber Swamp Side and adjoyneing to the Land of William Elcome East up the Said Swamp according to the Severall courses thereof 185 po: to a corner stooping marked white oake standing neare Mr. Sorrells path thence North Westerly 15 deg: 462 po: to a corner marked oake on a branch of Warrony Swamp thence North ... to a tree near an Indian feild thence North Westerly 32 deg: 108 po: to a corner marked Pockhiccory standing on Warrony Main Swamp thence

South Westerly down the said Swamp 305 po: to a corner marked birch tree belonging to Mr. Burwells Land and standing in Sr. John Aytons line thence a Long the said line South Easterly ... to a corner tree in William Elcomes line thence South along the Said Line 168 po: to the place where it began, which said Land was formerly granted to Mr. Henry Hartwell by patent, 30 May 1679 and by him deserted and after granted to Mr. Edward Chilton by order of Generall Court, 20 Nov. 1682, and by him deserted and never patented and since granted to Mr. William Edwards by order of Generall Court, 16 April 1690, and patented by patent, 23 Oct. 1690, and by him deserted and is now granted to the aforesaid Henry Duke Gent. by order of Generall Court, 2 Nov. 1693, and is due by and for the Importation of 15 psons, 20 April 1694.
Tho. Capwell   Rich'd. Stabbs   Susan: Ally
Cath Dunahon   Jack, Judith (as in the Ms.)
   Tony, ffrank, Jorny, Crocky, Boss, Betty, Negroes
     Three by cert. of E. Chilton Cl. Off.

p. 322.

Capt. Henry Duke, 90 acres, in Jas. City Co., bounded from his corner white oake on Tiascunn Swamp along the Line of his Land he purchased of William Manning South ... to an oake Sapplin on a Slash and down the Runh of the said Slash to Warrory Creeke and up the Same to Tiascun Bridge and thence up Tiascun Swamp to the first white oake, the said Land being due unto the said Capt. Henry Duke by and for trasportation of 2 psons., 20 April 1694.
The two: Daniel, Marreah, negroes.   Signed E. Andros

p. 323.

Mr. Edward Wade, 83 acres, Jas. City Co., bounded from John Hixes Corner Gum Standing on a branch of Warrany Swamp North 69½ deg: Easterly along the Land formerly Mr. Collins 13¼ cha: to a falen Spanish oake corner three thereof thence North North 59 deg: Easterly along Gammase foy (or toy) Land 17½ cha: to an oake on Rockahock path and up the said path to Warrony Land and along it North ... to another oake marked tree of the said Warrony Land thence South ... to a white oake and thence along Warrany Land again South ... to an old poplar stump on a branch and down it to the first mentioned branch of Warrany Swamp, and up the Runn thereof, to the place it began. The said Land being due unto the said Edward Wade by and for the Importation of 2 psons. 20 April 1694. Signed E. Andros
                     Two Negros.

p. 323.

Henry Thomson, 10 acres, Jas. City Co., bounded Vizt. begining at the Crossing of Rockahock and Hotwater Road and runing down hotwater Road to the marked line of hotwater Devident of Land and along it North ... to Rockahock road and down the Same to the first mentioned Crossing of the Roads, The Said Land Being due unto the Said Henry Thompson by and for the Importation of 1 pson. 20 April 1694.
Signed E. Andros.
                     One Negro.

p. 324.

John Young, Jas. City Co., 376 acres, beginning at a corner hiccory Mr. Robert Sorrell and Mathew Collins, thence by the said Collins his line North ... to an old corner Spanish oake neare a branch of Warrany, thence East by North ... to a corner red oake on the West side of old Rockahock path thence along the same the several courses thereof ... to the place where it first begann. The said 376 acres of Land was formerly granted unto James Bray and Thomas Hancock by patent, 18 April 1671, and by them deserted, and is since granted to the said John Young by order of the Generall Court, at James City, 25 Oct. 1693, and is further due by and for Importation of 8 psons. 20 April 1694. Signed E. Andros.

James Pollard	Thomas Graves	Tho: ffalk
Jane ffalk	John Jones	Mary Sorrell
	Sarah Hannot	

p. 384.

William Sherwood, Jas. City, Gent., 308 acres, In James City and James City Island, beginning on James River at the head of a branch of Pitch & Tarr Swamp next above the State house, and runing along the North side thereof to a Ditch dividing the Land of the said William Sherwood and the Land formerly belonging to one Thomas Woodhouse along the said Ditch South ... over the said branch of Pitch & Tarr Swamp to the 3½ acres of Land, which the said William Sherwood purchased of John Page Esq. and along the same, the said course, in all 23 cha: to a mulberry tree neere the Land of John ffitchett, thence South ... to the acre of Land the said William Sherwood purchased of David Nowell brother and heir at law of Jonathon Nowell dec'd. and along it South ... towards the dwelling house of Henry Hartwell Esq. thence North ... thence along the same acre, and the Land of the said William Sherwood which he purchased of the Said David Nowell as heir of the said Jonathon Nowell, Brother and the Creditors of the said Jonathon, South ... to the upper corner of the orchard belonging to one James Chesleigh and Ann his wife and along the said Ditch thereof, over a branch of Pitch & Tarr Swamp to the Lower corner of the said orchard thence East... to a gum of Pitch & Tarr Swamp, South ... to an oake in Mr. Travis's line and along it North ... to a pine on the South side of Pitch and Tarr Swamp, and down the said Swamp to a Dead oake on Pinney Point, thence over the said Swamp or Pitch and Tarr Marsh North ... to a gum in a sharp Point of Land thence over another Marsh North ... to a gum in a sharp Point of Land thence over another Marsh North ... to a point of swamp and along the North side thereof to a line of marked trees, and along it North ... to a corner oake of the Land formerly belonging to Richard James and along it North ... to - (space in the Ms.) Back river Marsh, and the same course 40 cha: through the Marsh to the river and up the same to Sandy Bay to a persimon tree under Block house hill thence under the said Hill West 6 cha: to James river, and down it to the head of the first mentioned branch, the said 308 acres of Land, being due, and belonging to the said William Sherwood as followeth, that is to say 3½ acres thereof Purchased of John Page by the said William Sherwood as appears by deed recorded in James City Co. Court, 6 Feb. 1681; 133 acres, 35 cha: 9 Dec. pts, the other pt. of the said 308 acres of land, being heretofore granted by patent, 6 May 1665, to one John Knowles, who conveyed the same to Jonathon Nowell all aforesaid and his heirs for Ever, 8 April 1668, and since purchased by the said William Sherwood of David Nowell brother & heir at Law of the said Jonathon Nowell and the trecitors of the said Jonathon, as by Severall Conveyances may appear; 28½ acres (other part of the said 308 acres formerly granted by patent, 4 Oct. 1656, to one John Baldwin who by his Last Will & Testament in writing under his hand and Seale did give same to one John ffulcher and his heires for Ever, and the said John ffulcher did by deed, 22 Oct. 1677, recorded in Jas. City Co. Court, sell and convey the same to the Said William Sherwood and his heires for Ever, the remaining of the said 308 acres of Land, being formerly granted to Richard James by Patent, 5 June 1657 and being Lately found to Escheat was granted to the said William Sherwood by patent, 23 Oct. 1690. Rec. 20 April 1694.

p. 395.

To all, etc. Whereas etc. and whereas a certain tract of Land lying in James City Co. and containing 150 acres late in the possession of Mark Bracket Dec'd., is lately found to Escheat ... Inquisition ... Henry Hartwell Esq. Escheator of the Said County ... 6 June 1693... which said Land Elizabeth Bracket the said Decease's Widow of this County ... granted unto Elizabeth Bracket the said 150 acres, 26 Oct. 1694.

p. 400.

Robert Beverley, 300 acres, 1 Rood & t po: of Land, Jas. City Co., bounded as followeth beginning at the Southermost End of the Ditch which Divided his from the Western side of the Lands Late of Lawrence (,) Coll. Bacon or one of them at the road Side extending Northward along the Ditch 36 2/5 po: to a slash called Pitch & Tarr Slash or Swamp then along up that slash till it come to the Maine cart road Westward makeing good in a right line 61 po: to the place it began the Said Land being due unto the Said Robert Beverley by and for the Imprtation of 1 pson. 26 Oct. 1694.
The Person: Isabella Markland. (Note: the acreage is possibly 30 acres.)

p. 407.

Capt. John Styth, 595 acres, Jas. City Co., bounded as followeth Upon the South side of Chickahominy river beginning at a marked white oake in Mr. Brumfeilds line of markt trees that standeth near a branch that runeth into Chicohamony river called the Great run where ffrancis Storey now liveth, thence West up the said branch to the head thereof, and further to a marked white oake 392 po: thence North West & by West to a great pine that standeth by a branch called Shaddocks branch thence ... to a corner white oake that stands by the Said Shaddocks branch being a corner tree of a former dividend of Mr. David Nowells thence South East and by East by a back line of the said Devident of Mr. Nowells & soe Continueing the same Course by a line of Mr. Brumfeilds Land to the white oake where it first begun that standeth by the aforesaid great run 661 po. This said land was formerly granted to William Broadribley, Patent Dated 6 Sept. 1665 and by him deserted, and was since granted to Benjamin Eggleston by Patent Dated 23 Oct. 1690 and by him deserted, and since granted to the said Capt. John Styth (by) order of the Hon:ble Generall Court, bearing Date at James City, 26 Oct. 1694 ... Importation of 12 psons. 21 April 1695.

Richard Smith	Antho. Comens	Edw'd Haskin
Wm. Choil	Tho: Powell	Jno. Barloe
Antho. Wellman	Ruth Williams	Jno. Chandler
Robert Davis	Andr. Barron	Dan:l Raven

p. 433.

Alexander Young of York County, a Devident of Land in Jas. City Co. near Wilmington Lower Church, 188 acres, bounded from James Hoods corner oake along his land South ... to an oake North ... to an oake and thence South ... to the first oake. The said 188 acres of Land being due to the said Alexander Young by purchase from John Major, 8 April 1689, to whom it was given by Last Will of Robert Morgan Son & heir of William Morgan to whom with other Lands it was granted by Patent, 21 April 1695. Note at the bottom of the patent: This patent hath a mistake, and is therefore recorded in the next leaf, according to ye originall. R. B. G. C.

p. 435. (Repeating from above)

... Alexander Young ... from James Woods corner oake along his land South ... to a Hiccory saplin thence along Morgans land North ... thence along ffishes Land North ... to an oake and thence South ... to the first oake ...

Bk. 9, p. 13.

William Wormeley Gent., Jas. City Co., 712 acres on the East side of Powhetan bounded from a great dead white oake below Powhetan Landing North ... to a poplar on the West side of Drinking Swamp and down the run of the said Swamp to a corner white oake on the East side thence along Wilkins Land North ... to an oake thence a long the Hon:ble Coll. Philip Ludwells Land North ... to drinking Swamp and down the run thereof to an old corner Elm on the West side the Said Swamp and along an old line South ... to Mr. Broadribbs corner stake & along his line South ... to a white oake on the South side of a great branch of Drinking Swamp thence South ... thence along through a narrow thickett (the partition of two feilds) South ... by an oake above a narrow point Landing of Powhatan and down Powhatan Creeke to the first mentioned white Oake, the said 712 acres of Land being due unto the said William Wormeley by and for Importation of 15 psons. 25 Oct. 1695. Signed E. Andros. (The persons are not named.)

p. 46

Dorcey Oatly one Island of Marsh Land, 126 acres, Jas. City Co., bounded Easterly by the Lower Gulf of Chicohamony River, and on all other parts by the Said River, said 126 acres of Marsh Land being due ... Importation of 3 psons. 29 Oct. 1696. Signed E. Andros.

Petition of Dorcy Oatly for 126 acres in Jas. City Co., E. Jennings Dept Sec'ry. The only name under the patent: Appia Sisly (or 2 Names.)

p. 49.

Lieut. Edw'd. Ross, Jas. City, whereon he now dwells, 5 Rood & 7 po: Bounding from a stake in the corner of an old Ditch near ye head of Pitch & Tarr Swamp Partly a Long the sd. Ditch North ... to James River Branch and Down it South ... to a stake in ye first mention(ed) Ditch and a Long it North ... to the first stake. (The acreage must be larger than above named.) 6½ acres of the sd. Land was formerly granted unto John Phips by Patent, 4 May 1661 and by him Deserted and Since granted unto ye said Lieut. Edward Ross by order of the Hon:ble Gen:ll Court, 15 April 1696 and ye residue being newly taken up and is due unto ye said Lieut. Edward Ross ... Importation of 1 pson. 29 Oct. 1696. The Person: Sam. Allen.

p. 51.

Thomas Nesham of James City Co., in upper part of the said County, 168 acres bounding from a white oake on ye West side of Nicketowaneos Path South ... to a hicory on ye West side of Dockmans run neare ye head thereof thence South ... a Long Peak's line to a pine, thence South ... to James River (als Bradffords) path and a Long it Easterwardly to Nickatowaneos Path and up that path to ye first white oake. The said 168 acres of Land being due ... Importation of 4 psons, 29 Oct. 1696.
Thomas Taylor, Eman'l. Dees, Booby, Tony.
    (Note: from Jas. City Co. Index: See No. 10, pa. 128.)

p. 89.

To all, etc. Whereas a certain Tract of Land Lyeing in Jas. City Co. and containing 867 acres late in possession of Thomas Wilkenson of the Said Co. dec'd. is lately found to Escheat ... Inquisition ... Dan:ll Park Esq. Escheator of the said County ... 6 March 1695/6 ... grant unto ye sd. Phillip Lightfoot the said 867 acres, 29 Oct. 1697. Signed E. Andros. E. __nings Dep. Sec.

p. 133.

Jas. City Co., 190 acres, late in the possession of John ffysher dec'd. is lately found to escheat ... Inquisition ... Dan:ll Parke Esq. Escheator for ye sd. County ... 18 Feb. 1696 ... Mrs. Angelica Bray of the said County ... grant to her, 190 acres ... 26 April 1698. Signed E. Andros.

p. 151.

Benj. Eggleston, Jas. City Co., on the East side of Powhatan Swamp, 1670 acres bounded from a ___ on the sd. Swamp in Mr. Broadribbs line along his land North ... to an oake on a branch of Drinking Swamp and up the said branch to a small oake on James Town Road and along the same 75 cha: to Mr. Phillip Indwells land and along it North ... to a hiccory near the North side of long meadow North ... to a white oake on the South Side of Rost pork Swamp then down ye side of the said Swamp to Personn (or Porsonn) corner white oake and along his land over the Said Swamp North ... to a saplin by a broken slump and North ... to a red oake on Powhatan Swamp & down the run or middle of the said Swamp so far as ye first mentioned Sally the Said land being due unto the Said Ben. Eggleston Vitz. 1377 acres by patent, 18 March 1662, and 293 the residue by an for transportation of 6 psons. 26 April 1698.

Kath. Teton   Jno. Haines   Will
ffran. Betterly   Tho. Roos   Sam

p. 161.

Mr. John Pettiver, Neck of Land, Jas. City Co., on the North side of Pease Hill Creeke, 43 acres, bounded from a white oake in a branch of the said Creeke in Sackville Brewers Line along the said Line North ... to Pease Hill Creek and down it to the mouth of the aforesaid branch and up the middle or water course of the said branch to the first white oake ye said Land being due unto ye said John Pettiver by and for transportation of 1 pson., 15 Oct. 1698. Signed E. Andros. The person: Timothy Lane.

p. 162.

Mr. William Edwards, 127 po: of Land Lying and being in James City Vizt., beginning from a slash on James River bank along the land Late of Tho: Rabley dec'd. North ... to a Slash and North ... to the Land his father William Edwards purchased of Henry Hartwell Esq. and along it South ... to a slash and South ... to the Land of Mr. James Chudley Lives on late belonging to Richard Holder dec'd. by patent, 28 Jan. 1672, and along the said Land South ... to a stake at ye mouth of the Orchard Run on James River thence North ... to the first stake of ye said Land being due unto ye said William Edwards ... transportation of 1 pson. 15 Oct. 1698. Signed E. Andros. Ed. Jenings, Dep. Sec. (The person not given.)

p. 184.

Matthew Williams, 200 acres, Jas. City Co., bounded (Vizt.) East on old Knights Land South on Mr. Morgan West on Philip Charles (,) Nicholas Goodale and John Merriman and North on the Maine branch of Warrany Creeke including 200 acres ... formerly granted unto William Hall, Sen'r. by Patent, 10 Feb. 1657 & by the sd. Hall sold & conveyed unto the sd. Matthew Williams and since renewed unto the said Matthew Williams by order of the Generall Court, 25 Oct. 1698, rec. 6 June 1699.
E. Jenings, Dept. Sec.   Signed ffra. Nicholson.

p. 232.

Thomas Wells, Jas. City, 34 perches, bounded from an old corner stake Capt. Marables upon bounds on James River a long his land and through his kitchen North ... to a stake on the South side of the Mill Roade and along it North ... to another stake neare the Cross Roade and thence by the East side thereof South ... to the first stake the sd. Land being due the sd. Thomas Wells ... transportation of 1 person, 26 Oct. 1699.   (Not named.)
E. Jenings, D. Sec.   Signed ffra Nicholson.

p. 240.

Tract of Land Lying in Jockies Neck in Jas. City Co., 135 acres late in the possession of John Wright, Dec'd. as Lately found to Escheat ... Inquisition ... Barth: ffowler Dep. Escheator to Philip Lightfoot Esq. Escheator Gener: fo the sd. County ... 17 Oct. 1698 ... appear for which sd. Land George Marable of the sd. County of Jas. City ... 135 acres ... 26 Oct. 1699.

69

E. Jenings, Dept. Sec.   Signed ffra Nicholson.

p. 425.

   Tract of Land, Jas. City Co., 370 acres, late in the possession of Mary Workman late daughter of Daniel Workman dec'd. is ... Escheat ... Inquisition ... 9 Sept. 1700 ... John Lightfoot Esq. Escheator ... Samuel Russell of the said County ... grant unto the said Samuel Russell, 24 Oct. 1701.
E. Jenings.   Signed ffr. Nicholson.

p. 509.

   Tract of Land, Jas. City Co., 27 acres, late in the possession of Jane Perkins dec'd ... Escheat ... John Lightfoot Esq. Escheator ... 1701/2 ... Wm. Woodward of Jas. City Co., hath made his composicon ... granted unto Wm. Woodward ... 28 Oct. 1702.
E. Jenings Sec.   Signed ffr. Nicholson.

p. 642.

   Tract of Land, Jas. City Co., 80 acres, late in the Possession of Thomas Pearson Dec'd. ... Escheat ... Inquisition ... John Lightfoot Esq. Escheator ... 14 April 1702 ... Benja: Pickett & Mary Short hath (as of the Ms.) made their composition ... granted unto Benja: Pickett & Mary Short, 20 Oct. 1704.
   C. C. Thacker Dep. Sec.

p. 658.

   William Barratt, 55 acres, Jas. City Co., the added part of a patent, 29 April 1692, by him deserted & is since granted unto the said William Barratt by order of the Gener:ll Court, 20 Oct. 1704 ... transportation of 2 psons., 2 May 1705. C C Thacker, Dep. Sec. Signed ffr. Nicholson. The 2 persons: Wm. Beebs & Rebecca Beebs.

p. 699.

   Edward Hooker, 412 acres in Wimbleto parish, Jas. City Co., bounded (Vitz.) beginning at a corner white oake in John Thomas's Line by the Great Swamp thence downe the said Swamp the severall courses to the Jones's Creek thence down the said Creeke to Lazarus Thomas his Creeke thence up the said Creek to Overmans line at the head of the sd. Creek thence along the sd. South ... to the place it began. 300 acres of this land was formerly granted by patent, 4 May 1638 unto Richard Hill and Roger Annwood and from them by several wills deeds and conveyances came to ye above sd. Edward Hooker & 112 acres found within the bounds of the abovesd. patent is due ... transportation of 3 psons., 2 Nov. 1705.
E. Jenings, Sec.   Signed Edw. Nott.
   The 3 persons: Geo. Harrison, Mary Sumers, Joanna Damon.

p. 716.

   Tract of Land, Jas. City Co., 130 acres, late in the possession of Peter Craw dec'd ... Escheat ... Inquisition ... John Lightfoot Esq. Escheat:r ... 18 Dec. 1699 ... Nazareth Whitehead orphan of Charles Whitehead of the Sd. Co., hath made his composition ... granted unto Nazareth Whitehead ... 1 May 1706
E. Jenings, Sec.   Signed Edw. Nott.

           Land Patents, in microfilm   Bk. 10, p. 1.

   For Importation of William Sherman ... grant & confirm unto John Wade, Jas. City Co., 47 acres, parish of We- (the microfilm is almost illegible) of Jas City & bounded as followeth (to wit) Begining at the mouth of a small gutt that Issueth out of James River called Warrons Quiver (?) thence South East by South South Easterly along lands of the said Quiver 82 po: to a branch that empties itself into the said James River just above William Whitacres upper Landing Dividing the Land from the Land of the said William Whitakre, Thence Running up the said Branch & North East & by East to the very head Spring thereof and to a small marked white oake standing on the North Side of the said Spring, Thence North ... to a small Locust Standing in a Gully at the head of a Small Branch falling into Warrons Run thence Down the said Branch and Run to the mouth thereof the beginning place first mentioned, 12 Dec. 1710.

p. 4.

21 April 1690, granted to John Soan of County of - (the space is in the Ms.) 82 acres, parish of -, on the West side of Chickahominy River in Jas. City Co., and bounded as followeth (to wit) Beginning from a corner white oake near Webbs Run along the bounds of his own Land South ... and thence to the first white oake North ... which said Tract or parcel of Land ... John Soan failed to make a seating and Henry Duke of Jas. City Esq. granted the said Land ... 28 April 1711.

p. 39.

Inquisition, Jas. City Co., Jas. City, 7 Aug. 1706, Warrant of John Lightfoot Esq. late our Escheator for the sd. Jas. City Co., Tract of land Commonly called Tutties Neck, 100 acres, is Escheat & Frederick Jones was granted it, 8 April 1711.

p. 76.

Philip Ludwell, Esq., Parish & Co. of Jas. City., 631 acres, on thw West side of Chicahominy River, bounded as followeth (to wit) Beginning at an old corner shrubby M:t oake upon ye West side of Nichettywans Path and running thence upon a New Line South ... to a small corner oak in the Easterly side of Dockmans Run near the head thereof thence along a part of the said Line - (illegible) the Line of Col. David Bray South ... upon a fair good Line of marked trees to a - of pines upon ye West side of Joriham (?) Path thence North East 4½ cha: to a small saplin oak and sd. oak standing between a marked oak & Hickory & White Oak being old marked trees Denoting a corner in this place thence ... first Line of marked trees (it - by a Jury in the year 1684 as the head bounds of Mr. George ffreemans Land) now the Line of the said Bray South ... to an ash on Joriham Run thence up and along it to the mouth of Long Branch and up it to an old corner red oak thence along a fair line of marked Trees dividing this from Kate Pattisons South West 159 cha: to a corner Pine up the East side (of) Nickettywans Path thence Down it to ye place it begun at 572 acres of the said Land are contained within ye bounds of 415 acres ... formerly granted to John Soan Dec'd. by Patent, 1683, and by several means & conveyances became the inheritance of the said Philip Ludwell and 59 acres residue of the said Tract of 631 acres are Queens Land Adjoining withall, 2 May 1713.
Signed A. Spottswood.

p. 93.

Simon Jeffreys of Jas. City Co., 167 acres lying and being on the West side of Chichahominy River in the Parish of Wilmington in the Co. of Jas. City and bounded as followeth, to wit, beginning at an old corner white oak standing in the fork of a little branch running out of the last side of Webbs Run thence on Thomas Rogers line South ... thence ... to two corner red oaks dividing this land from the land of Catherine Bennett (or Tennett) thence along this New Line North ... to Tobacco house run thence along it to Webbs run & up Webbs run to the first mentioned branch & up it to the place at ... 13 Nov. 1713.   Signed A. Spottswood.

p. 107.

George ffreeman Junior, 164 acres, Jas. City Co., upon West side of Chickahominy River & bounded as followeth, to wit, beginning on

Pease hill creek & running upon & along the line of Coll. David Poray North 79¼ West to a stake thence upon another of the said Porays lines North 29½ deg: & Westerly to a great forked red oak in the line of Mr. Thos. Cowles thence along this line ... thence upon & along the same creek till you come & are opposite to the house of George ffreeman Sen:r. then crossing the sd. Creek ... on Tinsley's line of old marked trees to a white oak on the head of Rags run thence bounding upon Stephen Dancy South ... to a hickory standing on the North Side of oags run aforesd. in ffrancis Dancy's line thence along the same Line & through Pease hill creek aforesaid ... thence South ... to another of the same Dancy's lines ... thence along the said creek to the place begun at ... 13 Nov. 1713.   Signed A. Spottswood

p. 121.

Inquisition "Taken at the Court house in the County of James City," 7 Feb. 1707, by warrant to Philip Ludwell, Esq., our Escheator for Jas. City Co., it appears that William Coleburn late of the sd. County of Jas. City died seized in fee of 50 acres of Land ... Escheat ... and whereas Joseph Wade of Jas. City Co. ... granted ... unto the said Joseph Wade ... bounded as followeth, to wit, geginning at an oak standing at the head of a branch of Webbs run thence along the upper bounds of Thomas Walter's land South ... to a stake thence West through the South corner of Thomas Walter's cornfield 53 cha: to two oaks on the East side of the first mentioned branch & up it to the head ... 13 Nov. 1713.   Signed A. Spottswood.

p. 128.

Inquisition, Jas City Co., 8 Dec. 1709, warrant of Philip Ludwell, etc., 168 acres ... Escheat to us from Thomas Nesham late of the said County, which by Patent granted to sd. Nesham, 29 Oct. 1706, bounded as followeth, to wit, from a white oak on the West side of Nickatewances path South ... to a hickory on the West side of Dockman's run near the head thereof thence South ... along Peak's line to a pine thence South ... to James River als Treadfords path & along it Eastwardly to Nickatewances path to the first white oak and whereas Daved Bray of Jas. City Co. ... grant ... David Bray ... 16 June 1714. (Porey is in the margin & also in the Index, but the text is unmistakably Bray in the last.)   See Bk. 9, p. 51 is at the foot of the patent. (From the Index: The date of the patent is in the year 1696.)

p. 131.

James Thomson Sen:r., 102 Acres, West side of Chickahominy River, beginning at the mouth of boyling Spring branch on pease hill run thence up the said branch to a corner pine upon the head thereof dividing this from Thomas Gouldsby's land thence South ... to Hitchcock's corner red oak thence along his line South ... to a corner pine so into pease hill run upon the same course & up it to the place begun at the sd. tract being part of 1250 acres formerly granted to Edward Cowles in 1661 but (not recorded) until the year 1711 upon the petition of Thomas Cowles Jun:r, to the General Court was conveyed by Capt. Thomas Cowles son & heir of the sd. dec'd. Edward to the sd. James Thomson in the year 1687 & rec. 16 June 1714.

p. 135.

David Davison, 304 acres, West side of Chickahominy River, Jas. City Co., bounded as followeth, to wit, beginning at the corner of a Ditch upon the Easterly side of the White meadow past Long Meadow at the mouth thereof upon the oaken Swamp thence up the middle of the sd. meadow & along the Ditch Dividing this from the land of Maj:r William Hunt to an old corner black oak upon the head thereof thence upon an old line of the sd. Hunt North ... to pease hill creek thence down it to a corner gum dividing this from the plantation of Mr. Thomas Cowles thence along a new dividing line between him and the sd. Cowles South ... to a stooping hickory and so into the side of the oaken swamp upon the same course & up the side thereof to the place begun at. The same being part of a patent of 1250 acres formerly granted to Edw'd. Cowles Dec'd by patent dated 1661 (But not recorded until 1711 upon the petition of Thomas Cowles Jun'r. to the General Court) and was conveyed by Thomas Cowles son and heir of the sd. Edward to Thomas Cowles and afterwards assigned by the sd. Cowles to David Davison Sen. Dec'd. father to the sd. Davison in the year 1682 & rec. 16 June 1714.

p. 145.

Robert Side, 400 acres, Jas. City Co., bounded as followeth to wit, beginning at a corner white oak in Necatewance in Wm. Pintts line thence along the sd. Pintt's line East ... to a corner hickory of Womsley's thence along Gilly's line South ... to the aforesaid Path where it began; which sd. Land is part of a patent of 900 acres granted to Roger Womsley, 18 March 1662 & by the sd. Side purchased of Edw'd. Gilly (who married the daughter of the sd. Womsley), 6 Aug. 1687 & rec. 6 June 1714.

p. 148.

Transportation of 6 psons: Rich'd Ball, Hen. Studdick, Ed. Powell, Ed. Carron, Perian Lashell & Rich'd. Hobert ... grant ... unto Simon Jefferys, 300 acres, West side of Chickahominy, Jas. City Co., bounded as followeth, to wit, beginning on the sd. River at a small cuprus in the mouth of a gutt dividing this from the land of John Goodale Dec'd. thence along his land West & by North ... to pease hill road being along the sd. Goodale's land now possest by John Shell (,) West by North ... to pease hill Creek Swamp & up the Middle of the same 160 cha: to the mouth of a branch & Up the Northerly branches of the same to an old marked pine in the head thereof thence East & by North by another old marked pine 31 cha: to a gum att the River Marsh & thence to the first mentioned cyprus, 16 June 1714.

p. 159.

John Hitchcock, 60 acres, West side of Chickahominy River, Jas. City Co., bounded as followeth to wit, beginning at a corner pine upon the head of a small branch of hogpen meadow thence down it to an old corner poplar scituate along the line of Mr. Rogers South ... to pease hill Run & so up it to Thomsons Corner red oak thence South ... to the place began, The same being part of a patent of 1250 acres formerly granted to Edw'd. Cowles Dec'd. in 1661 (but not recorded until the year 1711 & upon the petition of Thos. Cowles Jun'r. to the General Court) and is also part of a greater quantity conveyed by Capt. Thomas Cowles Son & heir fo the sd. Edw'd. Cowles to the sd. John Hitchcock who is in the quiet & peaceable possession of the sd. 60 acres by an agreement instead of the sd. greater quantity, 16 June 1714.

p. 159.

Thomas Young, 356 acres, North side of James River, Jas. City Co., & bounded as followeth, to wit, beginning at a corner hickory upon the River, dividing this from the land of Richard Moyses & thence along the Line of Nicholas Moyses & Mr. Blaikley North ... to Mr. Blaikley's his corner red oak thence upon the same course ... to John Watson's corner stake thence on the same course ... thence down the River along an old line dividing this from Thomas Denkins South ... thence along the River to the place begun: The sd. land being part of a patent formerly granted to Thomas Swan Esq. for 500 acres, 18 Dec. 1668, and by several - (one word illegible) & conveyances is become the inheritance of the sd. Thomas Young, 16 June 1714.

p. 162.

Patent, 25 Oct. 1687, was granted to John Soane, 66 acres, on the upper side of Pease hill Creek, Jas. City Co., and bounded as followeth to Wit., beginning at Pease hill run at a line of marked trees belonging to Potters field Devident of land and along it North ... to

Pease hill run & up it to the first mentioned line: which said tract or parcel of land was granted on condition of seating & planting of the sd. patent and whereas the sd. John Soane hath failed to make such seating & planting and Simon Jeffrey of the said County of Jas. City hath made humble suit ... Importation of two psons. ... whose names are Sam. Remble and Thomas Lee ... Granted ... unto the said Simon Jeffreys, 16 June 1714.

p. 169

Thomas Goulby, 195 Acres, West side of Chichahominy River, Jas. City Co., and bounded as followeth, to wit, beginning at the mouth of boyling spring branch of Pease hill run thence up and along the sd. branch to corner pine on the head thereof thence upon an old line North ... thence ... Westerly upon Mr. Cowles line 20½ cha: to Hint's (?) corner oak thence along his line South ... Easterly along Hinds (?) line ... to Pease hill creek and so down to the place begun at. The said Tract being of a patent formerly granted to Edward Cowles dec'd. for 1250 acres dated 1661 (but not recorded until the year 1711 upon the petition of Thomas Cowles Jun:r by the General Court) and was conveyed by Capt. Thomas Cowles son & heir of the said Dec'd. Edward Cowles to Thomas Gouldby dec'd. father to the sd. Gouldby in the year 1685 & rec. 16 June 1714.

p. 169.

Inquisition, Jas. City Co., 8 Dec. 1709, 300 acres of Land lying and being in the parish of Wallingford in the sd. Co. ... Escheat ... Whereas Thomas Young hath made humble suit ... Survey ... by Simon Jeffreys Survey of the said County, 30 March 1710 is found to contain 372 acres ... granted ... unto the sd. Thomas Young ... on the North side River ... bounded as followeth, to wit, at a great corner Pine upon the - one word, illegible, of the long Thicket and running down the same ... thence upon John Hawby's land ... to a corner white oake thence on Mr. Lightfoot's line South ... to a corner pine thence on Thomas Ebberle's head line North ... to his corner red oak thence on Mr. Blaikley's line of new marked trees North ... to the corner red oak in Young's line (formerly Rumbal's) thence North ... to a stake thence North ... on Watson's new line ... to the place began at ... 16 June 1714.

p. 179.

Inquisition, Jas. City Co., 13 Aug. 10 Anne, Warrant to Philip Indwell(?) Esq., our Escheator for the sd. County of Jas. City. It appears that John Were late of the said County of Jas. City died seized of 200 acres of Land (more or less) ... Excheat ... whereas Nicholas Valentine of the sd. County of Jas. City hath made humble suit ... survey ... by Simon Jeffrey Surveyor ... last Oct. 1713 is found to contain 240 acres. Therefore ... granted unto the sd. Nicholas Valentine ... in the parish of Wilmington, in the County of Jas. City and bounded as followeth, to wit, beginning at the mouth of Morgan's Swamp thence up a branch thereof dividing this from the land of Mr. Tho. Cowles dec'd. to a corner hickory upon the head thereof thence upon an old line dividing this from Capt. Norwell's North ... to a Spanish oak a corner of this, John Bash & the sd. Norwell thence on Bashis(?) line South ... to an oak upon Morgan's Swamp thence along the water course thereof as it windeth Easterly to a Spanish oak thence South 2 deg: Lasterly along a Line of marked trees dividing this from Bash 79¼ cha: to a corner white oak upon the side of Jones Swamp thence along the water course thereof as it tendeth Westerly to the place begun at by a narrow point of land where Morgans & Jones Swamp forkes: 16 June 1714.

p. 191.

Importation of 5 psons: Rich'd Roberts, Rich'd. Peall, Henry Shaddock, Ed. Powell & Ed. Carron ... granted ... unto John Woodward, 230 acres, on East side of Chicohominy River, parish of Wilmington, Jas.

City Co., bounded as followeth, to wit, beginning at an old corner xx oak on the East side of Diascun Swamp dividing this from the land of one Edmonds thence on his old line North ... thence on Mr. James Duke's line North ... to Warran Eye Swamp side, so through it to include the same & so down the North Westerly side including the whole swamp to a short markt line below the sd Woodward's mill running North ... between the sd. swamp & birchen Swamp, so through birchen Swamp on the same course & down the North Westerly side thereof to include it to its mouth on Deascun Swamp thence down the water run of Diascun Swamp to the intersection with the first mentioned course & line and thro' the swamp up upon the same course to the corner begun at, 16 June 1714.

p. 221.

Importation of 4 psons.: Richard Phillip, John Speed, Thos. Atkinson, & Jno. Elliot ... granted unto Robert Goodrich, 170 acres, South side of Checkerhouse Creek and the main Eastwardly branch thereof comonly called Scotland Swamp (and divideth his from Coll. Robt. Holt's Land) on the East side of Chichahominy River in the parish of Wilmington in the County of Jas. City and bounded as followeth, to wit, beginning at the mouth of a branch of the sd. Checkerhouse Creek called Titus Gut thence up it 50 cha: upon a straight line to a Thicket of marked saplines of several sorts of trees thence on a new line dividing this from the Land of Coll. Lidwell East 148 cha: to an ash & maple by the mouth of a little gully on the West side of a branch & by the head thereof West to and in sight of James Town main Road thence down that branch ... to his sd. Easterly branch called Scotland Swamp and down it to the place begun at, 23 Dec. 1714.

p. 222.

Importation of 1 pson.: Mathew Whis (?) ... granted ... unto John Bush, 1034 acres, in Wilmington parish, Jas. City Co., and bounded as followeth, to wit. beginning at the Spring on the head of Jones Swamp, thence down and along his said Swamp to a corner white oake on the side thereof thence on a new line dividing this from the land of Nicholas Valentine North ... to a Spanish oak upon the South side of a branch of Jones Swamp thence on that branch as it tendeth Westerly ... thence along a new Line dividing this from the sd.Valentine's North ... thence along another new Line North North East ... thence upon an old Line of the sd. Bush North ... to a corner Spanish oak dividing this from the Land of the sd. Valentine & Capt. Newell, thence a long an old Line of the sd. Bush's North ... to a hickory on the Southermost main branch of warron-eye Creek thence North ... to a branch of Warren-eye Creek thence up it to an old markt hickory at the very head thereof thence South ... to the mainroad that goes down the County thence along it East ... thence upon an old Line of the sd. Bush's South ... thence down that Line North ... to the place begun at. 317 acres of the sd. Tract was formerly granted to Nicholas Bush dec'd. by patent dated 1655 from whom it legally descended to the sd. John Bush and 37 acres of the sd. Tract is Surplusage within the bounds of the sd. Patent and 680 acres residue of the sd. Tract is part of a patent of 809 acres, 16 cha: & 5 dec. pts of land formerly granted to Joseph Knight in 1665 who devised the same in two different parcels between the sd. John Bush & his brother Joseph Bush by his last Will & Testament dated in Feb. 1676 & rec. 23 Dec. 1714.

p. 228.

Importation of 2 psons.: Derrick Anderson & Nicholas Rennffee ... grant ... unto Nicholas Moyses, 90 acres, North side of James River whereon he now lives in Wallingford parish, Jas. City Co., and bounded as followeth, to wit, beginning at Mr. Young's corner hickory upon the River & running from thence on his Line North ... to a gum on the side of a Slash, thence on Mr. Baikley's dividing Line of old marked trees South ... to a Dog oak saplin in another line of the sd. Blaikley's, thence down it South ... to a corner pine saplin upon the River thence up it to the place begun at. The aforesaid Tract being within the reputed bounds of 50 acres more or less as the ½ of a

75

tract sold and conveyed in the year 1687 by Wm. Wilkins to James Haly & William Colgil for 100 acres more or less as part of a patent of 1900 & odd acres formerly granted to Petre Hoe which sd. half containing aforesd. 90 acres is by several mean conveyances come to the possession of sd. Nicholas.   23 Dec. 1714.

p. 230.

Catherine Barrett, 400 acres, West side of Chichahominy River, parish of Wilmington, Jas. City Co., and bounded as followeth, to wit, beginning at an old corner beech by the marsh side of the sd. River & runneth upon a new line dividing this from Sachfeild Brewers' Land & the Land of Simon Jeffrey's South ... thence upon another new Line being the uppermost bounds dividing this from the Land of the sd. Jeffreys South ... to two corner red oaks thence upon a new Line dividing this from Henry Gilbert's Land North ... into & through the marsh to the Intersection of a course or straight Line to the run, taken or observed from the very mouth of Raroper branch on the aforesd. River to the aforesd. beech thence along & through the marsh upon the River on that same course or straight Line to the said Beech begun at. The sd. 400 acres being part of a patent of 850 acres formerly granted to Wm. Barrett Dec'd. in June 1648 from whom it legally descended to James Barrett Dec'd son & heir of the sd. Dec'd. Wm. Barrett 800 acres of which sd. Tract was by the Last Will & Testament of the sd. James Barrett given & devised to the sd. Catherine & Edith now wife of the sd. Gilbert to be equally divided between them.   23 Dec. 1714.

p. 237.

Importation of Henry Rogers ... grant ... unto William Marable, Jas. City Co., one certain triangular Island of Marsh, 13 acres, invironed with Archer's hope creek, Northerly side of the Southermost branch of the sd. Creek & below, adjoins & is opposite to the mouth of the Southerly branch (issuing out of the sd. Creek) that bounds Mr. Marables Jockey's Neck Land on the South side thereof. 16 Aug. 1715.

p. 249.

Importation of 5 psons.: Wm. Bear, Henry Matherod, Henry Heathrosh & Josias Bone (all given) ... granted ... unto Martine Sorrell, 280 acres, Wilmington parish, Jas. City Co., (being the plantation whereon he now lives) and bounded as followeth, to wit, beginning at the mouth of a little gut running out of the East side of a branch of Timber Swamp, thence along Coll. Duke's Line North ... to a Spanish oak upon the road that goes down the Country from the Coll.'s house, thence along that Road (being the dividing bounds between his & Mr. Ballard's) according to its several courses ... thence along South ... to Mr. Sorrell's corner hickory, thence along his line North ... to a branch of Timber Swamp, thence along that branch as it headeth Northerly 40 cha: to the place begun.   80 acres of the sd. Tract is part of a patent of 497 acres formerly granted to Richard Humbek and is now the Inheritance of the sd. Martin Sorrell and 200 acres residue of the sd. Tract is Surplusage Sand within the bounds of the sd. 80 (acres).   16 Aug. 1715.

p. 250.

Henry Gilbert, 400 acres, West side of Chichahominy River, in the parish of Wilmington, Jas. City Co., and bounded as followeth, to wit, beginning at two corner red oaks in his woods being a corner of his, the land of Simon Jeffreys, thence along a new line of 850 acres of w:ch this is a part (the solid & ancient bounds being utterly unknown) South ... to a red oak and two maples on the run side of the Lower or Easternmost branch of Raroper Swamp, thence down that swamp and branch to the mouth thereof on Chichahominy River, thence on a straight Line or course that will exactly butt or take an old Reputed corner beech of his sd. 850 acres which standeth by the marsh side of the sd. River and is a corner of the Land of Catherine Barrett and

Sachfield Brewer so far upon the sd. straight Line or course of
Kath'n. Barret which divideth her Lands from his thence on her
dividing course and New Line South ... to the corner two red oaks
begun at. The sd. 400 acres being part of a Patent of 850 acres
aforesd. was formerly granted to Mr. Wm. Barrett dec'd. in June 1648
from whom it legally descended to Mr. James Barrett dec'd son & heir
of the sd. dec'd. Mr. Wm. Barrett, 800 acres of w:ch sd. tract was by
the Last Will & Testament of the sd. James Barrett given and devised
to Edith now wife of sd. Gilbert and the sd. Katherine Barrett to be
equally divided between them his lawful daughters; and upon a Survey
of whole and divisions thereof made according to the will of the sd.
dec'd. Mr. James Barrett the sd. 400 acres surveyed and bounded as
aforesd. was chosen by the sd. Gilbert in Right of his sd. wife and
bounded as aforesd. at his request as it is said ... 16 Aug. 1715.

p. 252.

John Holloway of Williamsburg, Gent., 833 square foot of Land from
Archer's hope creek at the Landing belonging to the City of Williamsburg called Princess or Princess Ann Port which he hath erected into
a wharfe convenient for Landing and taking of goods into Boats, Sloops
and other vessels to the great advantage of the present & future
Inhabitants of the sd. City of Williamsburg; which sd. 833 sq. ft. of
Land are below the high water mark at the sd. Landing or Port where
Tide did formerly flow and which parcel of Land or new raised wharf
containing 833 sq. ft. below high water mark is described in a Platt
which was made upon a Survey of the sd. landing or Port by Ch:rs Jackson Surveyor of the sd. City of W:msburg, 24 Aug. 1715, and is
described in that platt by four Letters pppp. We have given & granted
... unto the sd. John Holloway, Gent., 8 Nov. 1715.

p. 317.

William Macklin, 200 acres, West side of Chichahominy river in the
parish of Wilmington, Jas. City Co., bounded as followeth, to wit,
beginning at the mouth of Brierly branch on the North side (of)
Moses run thence down Mosses run as it tendeth Easterly to a corner
red oak dividing this from the land of William Adams along a new
dividing line between this & the land of the sd. Adams North ... to a
red oak thence along a new line dividing this from the land of Maj:r
Wm. Hunt South ... to an ash on the head of Briery branch aofresd.
thence down it to its mouth begun at the said Land being part of a
patent of 1250 acres formerly granted to Edward Cowles dec'd. by
patent 1661 but not recorded until 1711 upon the petition of
Thomas Cowles Jun:r to the Gen:ll Court & by several means & convey-
ences is become the Inheritance of the said Macklin. 1 April 1717.

p. 317.

James Jennings, 439 acres, parish of Wilmington, Jas. City Co.,
bounded as followeth, to wit, beginning at the mouth of Capt. Cowles
mill creek on Warran Eye Creek thence up the Marsh side of Warran
Eye Creek and the Creek itself where it comes into the High Land to
the bottom of a Neck opposite to the mouth of back creek thence round
the Neck and up the marsh side of the said creek & the sd. Creek itself
where it comes into the high land to the mouth of Toneys Swamp upon the
said Creek thence up Toney's Swamp and cross the road (from the said
Cowles Mill to Diascun bridge) to Coll. Birds line of Land formerly
patented by Mr. Soan Thence down that line South ... to Cowles Corner
Dogwood thence up the same course along the line of the said Cowles ...
thence upon the dividing line between this and the land of Edward
Green South ... to a little branch runing out of the said Cowles mill
creek thence down it to the said creek thence down that creek to the
beginning. 160 acres of the said Land is part and half of a patent
of 320 acres called Hill Neck formerly granted to Edward Cole in 1661
(probably a mistake for E. Cowles) and by several means & conveyances
is become the Inheritance of the said Jennings. 225 acres part of ye
residue of the said tract in Surplusage land within the bounds of the
said patent and half of the said patent and the 54 acres full residue

of the said Tract is Surplusage land within the bounds of the other half and part of the aforesaid patent in the possession of Edward Green who relinquished his privilege to the said Surplusage within the bounds of the said half and part to the said James Jenings. 15 July 1717.

p. 341.

Thomas Atkinson, 64 acres, in Martins hundred, Jas. City Co., bounded as followeth, to wit., beginning at a crooked poplar standing on the East side of a Swamp dividing this tract from Thomstons Land thence down the water course of the said Swamp to the marsh to the Eastermost side thereof thence upon a long & round the sides & heads of several points of marsh to the mouth of Ramseys run which divides the tract from Grices Land thence up the said run to a Sweet gum near the head thereof thence North and by East ... to the place begun at which said tract of Land is part & parcel of 185 acres formerly granted to Richard Whittaker by Patent, 1666, and by him conveyed to David Crawford in the year 1669 and by the said Crawford conveyed to Thomas Atkinson dec'd., 1679, and given by the Last Will & Testament of the same Atkinson, 1709, to the above mentioned Thomas Atkinson his son. 15 July 1717.

p. 408.

William Murray, 235 acres, parish of Wallingford, Jas. City Co., bounded as followeth, to wit, Beginning at a corner gum upon the Westerly side of the long thicket and running from thence South ... to an oak along an old crooked line dividing this from the land of Edward Clipon thence South ... to a corner white oak along an old crooked line dividing this from the land of William Clark and Joseph Parish thence along an old line dividing this from the land of John Watson North ... to an old corner white oak near the long thicket thence along a new line North ... through the long thicket to a Sally and white oak thence along another new line up the long thicket dividing this from the land of George Hunt North ... to the first mentioned gum. 200 acres of which said tract of land is part of a patent of 400 acres formerly granted by patent, 6 Aug. 1655 to Thomas Jones and 35 acres the residue to the said tract is surplusage land within the bounds of the said 200 acres as part of the aforesd. patent 22 Jan. 1718.

p. 415.

Inquisition, Jas. City, 11 Sept. 1717 ... It appears that Mihil Goen late of the said County of Jas. City dyed seised of 30 or 40 acres ... Escheat ... Survey, 24 Nov. 1708, by Christopher Jackson Surveyor of Jas. City Co., is found to contain 37 acres and whereas Robert Hubbard of the aforesaid County of Jas. City hath made humble suit ... granted ... unto the said Robert Hubbard ... in Yorkhampton parish, Jas. City Co., and bounded as followeth, to wit, beginning at a corner between Mihil Goen (,) Robert Hubbard & ffrancis Moreland and runing South ... to a beach tree standing at the head of beach Spring it being a corner tree between Graves Pack, ffrancis Moreland and Michael Gowen the person from whom this land is escheat thence down the said beach Spring branch according to the meanders thereof until it meets with Green Swamp thence up the said Swamp according to the sundry courses thereof unto a place called the horse bridge thence South ... to the place begun at. 22 Jan 1718.

p. 461.

Inquisition, Jas. City Co., 11 Sept. 1717 ... It appears that Edward Ridley son of Peter Ridley late of the said County of Jas. City dyed seised of 50 acres ... and whereas ffrancis Moreland and Anne his wife of the aforesaid County of Jas. City have made humble suit ... granted ... unto ffrancis Moreland and Anne his wife ... being in the parish of Merchants Hundred and County aforesaid and bounded as followeth, to wit, beginning at a great Spanish oak on on Sanders marsh along the bounds of the land of Littler deed (?) South ... to an ash in another branch thence South Easterly to a white oake saplin on cold Spring run & down the same to a branch of Keiths Creek called back creek run and up the said run to the mouth of the run of Sanders Marsh and up the Same to the first Spanish oak. 20 Feb. 1719.

Bk. 11, p. 32.

Inquisition, Jas. City Co., 11 March 1717, Edmund Jennings Esq. the Escheator for the said County, It appears that John Smith late of the said County died seized of 114 acres ... Escheat ... 11 April 1718 by Christopher Jackson surveyor of the said County is found to contain 192 acres, and whereas Robert Goodrich of the County aforesaid ... granted ... 192 acres ... (being part of Hotwater dividend) and bounded as followeth, to wit, Beginning at a Small ash tree standing on a branch of Checkerhouse Creek near Lambeths corner thence North ... ... to a Spanish oak standing on the side of Hookers mill road which said 3 courses distances divides the lands belonging to the orphans of Benjamin Goodrich dec'd. from this thence along the said road North ... thence crossing the said road & continuing the sd. Course ... to a shrub white oak thence North ... to the head of a valley being a corner between the lands of Phillip Ludwell Esq. (,) Robert Porteus Esq. (,) the said Robert Goodrich and distant from the Spring in the said valley 58 years which 4 last courses parts the land of Robert Porteus Esq. from this thence up the said valley North ... to Hooker's mill road thence crossing the sd. road down a great valley South ... to the said run of Checkerhouse Creek branch (which 6 last mentioned courses divides the lands of Phillip Ludwell Esq. from this) and so along down the said branch according to the meanders thereof to the beginning. 17 Aug. 1720.
Marginal note: 192 Escheat land   Signed A. Spotswood.
form, in 104th page of the book before
this. (If Bk. 10 is meant, not there.)

p. 97.

Inquisition, Jas. City Co., 1 Nov. 1720 a Warrant directed to Edmond Jenings Esq. Escheator of the said County of Jas. City, It appears that Ralph Fustain late of said Co. of Jas. City died Seized of 50 acres of land ... Escheated ... survey ... 21 Dec. 1721 by Christopher Jackson Surveyor of the said Co. ... whereas Robert Ashurst of the said Co. ... Beginning at a saplin oak and running from thence North ... to a Sallow near the said Ashurst's spring thence down the said spring branch according to the meanders thereof till it meets with the main run thereof to a white oak being a corner tree between this land and Benjamin Pichetts land thence along the line Dividing this land from Benjamin Pichetts South ... to a Sallow being a marked tree in the said line and now made a corner of the said Ashursts land from thence North ... through the old field 94 po: to the beginning. 22 June 1722. Signed A. Spotswood.

p. 236.

Inquisition, Jas. City Co., 21 Nov. 1720, Warrant from Edmund Jenings, Esq., then the Escheator for the said Co. of Jas. City, It appears that George Barker late of the said Co. of Jas. City dyed seised of 51 acres of Land in Jockies Neck ... Escheat ... Christopher Jackson ('s survey) ... contains 50 acres, 52 po: ... Philyp Ludwell of sd. County of Jas. City Esq. hath made humble suit ... granted ... unto the said Phillip Ludwell ... Beginning at a Red oak standing on a Point and extending itself along a small Swamp North ... to a marked oak dividing this Land from the Secretaries Land and thence along the said line cross the Oldfield into the woods South ... to a marked red oak at the Edge of the woods Thence South ... on the West side of a Small run Thence South ... to a corner oak standing near where two Runs meet thence down thereof to the first Westerly branch of Archer's hope Creek thence up the said Branch according to the meanders thereof to the Swamp that divides the Land now in the occupation of William Marable from this Land and so up the Said Swamp according to the

meanders thence & to the Beginning. 5 Sept. 1723.
    Marginal note: the same   Signed Hugh Drysdale.
    ref. as above to 104th page
    of book before this.

Bk. 13, p. 378.

Inquisition, Jas. City Co., 3 Feb. 1727, William Byrd Esq. the then Escheator of the said Co. of Jas. City, It appears that Elizabeth Hoy late of the said Co. of Jas. City died Seized of 300 acres of Land, Parish of James City, Co. of Jas. City ... Escheat ... 4 April 1728, Survey by William Comrie Surveyor of the sd. County ... containing 309 acres, and whereas John Hoy of Jas. City County ... granted ... unto the said John Hoy, being in the ffork between pagan Creek and Youngs Creek on Checkorees Creek (?, and on) Chickahoming (? River) in James City Co. ... (formerly belong(ing) to Job. Bellamy Dec'd.) and bounded as followeth, to wit, Beginning at a Gunn on the head of Cross Creek from thence South ... to a pine on the head of a Branch Thence down the water course of the Said Branch untill it Joines with Pagan Creek down the Said Creek untill it meet(s) with Younges Creek Then up Youngs Creek to the mouth of Cross Creek then up the water course of the said Creek to the Gunn first station. 11 Aug. 1729.
                    Signed William Gooch

Vol. 14, p. 9. (No County Index.)

(Philip Smith of Williamsburg one certain Tract or parcel of Marsh Land lying and being on Chickahominy River and know by the name of Ox Island and Bird Island, 37 acres, 28 Sept. 1728. (Description is omitted. The record may not be of Jas. City Co.))

p. 317.

Thomas Green of Gloucester Co., 801 acres, in the Middle Branch of Warrany in Jas. City Co. and bounded as Followeth (to wit) Beginning at the center of a Red Oak (,) a black scrub by Oak Saplin and a hiccory saplin Running North North West 240 po: to a hiccory Tree on the North side (of) Coles Mill Road From Thence North ... to a white oak on the Rowon (?) Spring Branch from Thence down the Water course of the said Branch Till it Joynes The Timber Swamp Thence down the Swamp to two white gums at the mouth of a Branch near the Bridge Thence up the said Branch South ... to the head of another Branch Thence down the Run of the said Branch holding course of The Marked Line ... Thence down the said Branch till it Joyns the mill Swamp Then up the said Swamp to the mouth of a Branch a little Below the Going Over Place Thence up the Branch to the First Station whic is on the head of the said Branch. 571 acres Part of the said Land being Surplus Land Found within the Bounds of a Patent granted to one Robert Sorrell, 20 Nov. 1653, for 700 acres and the Residue being Parcel of 700 acres The Right whereof is vested in the Said Green by Diverse Mesine conveyances. 5 Aug. 1731.

p. 364.

Inquisition, Jas. City Co., 22 Dec. 1726, warrant to Edmund Jennings, Esq. the then Escheator ... It appears that Elizabeth Marable late of the said Co. of Jas. City died seized of two plantations called the New Ordinary and Thomsons, Jas. City Co., ... Escheat ... survey, 31 May 1728, by William Couris (or Comris) Surveyor of the said County of Jas. City are found to contain 147 acres of Land ... grante ... unto William Marable ... in Jas. City Parish and Co. formerly belonging to Doctor Cherineson and bound as followeth, to wit, Beginning at a Red Oak on the Maine County Road being the Sign Tree of the New ordinary from that up the Road North ... to an old stump side then South ... to a white oak at the head of a Run that goes down to Blue Gaps hole then down the meanders of the said Run till it joyns the head Spring branch Swamp then down the Said Swamp to the mouth of a Branch then up a Line of old Marked Trees South ... to a large hiccory on the hagpen Meadows then up the Swamp of the said Meadows to a white oak at the head thereof Then North ... to the ffirst Station. 17 Sept. 1731.

(Continuation of the Land Records) Bk. 19, p. 662.

Inquisition, Jas. City Co., 24 April 1727, warrant to Edmund Jennings, Esq., our Escheator for the said Co., It appears that William Ellis formerly of the Co. of New Kent died seised of a certain Tract or Parcel of Land containing 195 acres & 2 po: Jas. City Co., ... Escheat ... and whereas Katherine Bacon Burwell hath made Humble Suit ... granted to Anne Hyde and Rebeckah Hyde, being bounded as followeth, to wit, Beginning at a red oak standing on a branch of Jones' Creek and running down the said branch the several courses the reof to a fork of the said Creek Thence up an other branch of the said Creek the several courses thereof to a white oak standing near the branch Thence crossing the neck to the beginning ... being part of the said quantity of 195 acres & 2 po: ... to be held of Anne Hyde & Rebeckah Hyde ... as of our mannor of East Greenwich in the County of Kent in fee and common soccage and not in Capite or by Knights Service. 10 June 1740.

p. 816.

Inquisition, Jas. City Co., 22 Nov. 1720, Warrant to Edmund Jennings, Esq., then Escheator ... Samuel Boys late of the Co. aforesaid died seised of a certain Tract or Parcel of Land containing 198 acres ... Escheat ... Whereas John Doran hath made humble suit to James Bkaurm Clerk President of our Council and Commander in Chief of our Colony ... grant ... Thomas Hilliard, Bounded as followeth, to wit, Beginning at the mouth of a valley that runs out of Arrow Reed branch and running Thence along a line of marked trees South ... to the mouth of Celler run and running Thence along the said run North ... to Henry Soan's line Thence along the said line North ... to Robert Wade's line formerly Joseph Wade's line Thence along the said line North ... of Highland to a corner gum in Duke's line and Thence along that line down the branch according to the meanders thereof to the mouth of Arrowreed branch the two branches meeting so as to make a point of highland look like an Equilateral triangle and so up the said Arrowreed branch according to its meanders to the first Station. 1 Dec. 1740.

Vol. 31, p. 635.

Inquisition, Jas. City Co., 6 April 1750, Warrant to Peter Randolph, Esq., our Escheator of the said Co. It appears that William Arminger died seised of a Lott or half acres of Land lying & being in James Town on the North side of James River in the said Co. which is found to escheat to us from the said William Arminger and Whereas Edward Champion Travis hath made humble suit ... granted ... unto the said Edward Champion Travis bounded as followeth, to wit, Beginning at high water mark at the said River where is a stone to be planted on the Bank near the Place running thence North ... Thence South ... thence through the said Travis' garden South ... to the said River at high water mark as aforesaid Thence up the said River North ... to the Beginning place. 10 Sept. 1755.

p. 731.

Richard Tyree, 509 acres, Jas. City Co., bounded as followeth, to wit, Beginning at a red oak and running thence North ... East ... North ... West ... North East ... North ... West .... Etc. ... to the Beginning. 225 acres part thereof formerly granted unto Thomas Rolfe and 284 acres the residue never before granted. 10 Sept. 1755.

(Continuation of the Land Records.) Bk. 33, p. 380.

Daniel Porter, 230 acres, Jas. City Co., bounded as followeth, to wit Beginning at an Ash on the South side of Cheekroes Swamp in Col. Philip Ludwell's line running thence down the said Swamp at its meanders and binding on the same to the mouth of Hotwater Swamp and thence continuing down the said Cheekroes Swamp binding on the same to the mouth of Cowheel Swamp thence up the said Cowheel Swamp as it meanders binding on the same to an Ash standing in the said Philip Ludwell's line by the side of the said Swamp thence along the said Lidwell's line North ... to a Posimon the South side of Hotwater Swamp thence up the said Swamp North ... to an Ash corner to the said Philip Ludwell and the said Porter on the South side of the said Swamp thence North 226 po: to the beginning. 29 Aug. 1757.

p. 419

Joshua Jones, 75 acres, Jas. City Co., and bounded as followeth, to wit Beginning at a red oak on the South side of Jefferys Branch formerly called and know by the name of the Ozyer Branch just below the head thereof at a fore and aft Tree in James Dilliard's line running thence along the said Dilliard's line South ... to the Intersection of this line with an ancient line of the Land formerly belonging to Col. Bray on the East side (of) the Middle Branch just below the head the reof along that line of marked Trees North ... to Isaac Goding's line thence along this line South ... to a small branch thence down that Branch binding on the same to the mouth thereof at the South Swamp thence down the said South Swamp binding on the same along side of Richard Glazbrooks Land and Burnell Jones' Land to the mouth of Jeffery Branch aforesaid thence up the said Branch as it meanders binding on that likewise to the beginning. 10 Nov. 1757.

p. 530.

James Dillard, 269 acres, in the counties of Jas. City & New Kent & bounded as followeth, to wit, Beginning at the Intersection where one of the Disputed lines falls in with Isaac Goddins line North ... to the head of a Branch running thence down the said Branch its several meanders binding on the same to Brays Swamp, thence down the several courses of the said Swamp passing Herds line to Rockahock Path, thence along the said Path binding on the same to Herds Patent line (now Allens) thence along that line South ... to Warrany Road, thence down the said Road binding on the same to a large red oak on the South side thereof thence North ... to the head of Jeffery's Branch, thence down the said Branch its several courses to the South Swamp & thence up the said Swamp as it meanders binding on the same to the mouth of a small Branch, thence up the said Branch to the said Goddins line and thence along his line North ... to the Beginning. 94 acres part thereof being Surplus Land found within the bounds of a former Patent the Right whereof is since become vested in the said Dillard. 15 Dec. 1758.

Vol. 34, p. 945.

Inquisition, Jas. City Co., 14 July 1760, ... It appears that Anne Vobe died seised of about 90 acres of Land, Jas. City Co., ... Escheat Whereas Alexander Finnie hath made humble suit ... granted ... unto Alexander Finnie ... bounded as followeth, to wit, Beginning at a stake in the Fork of A Swamp and running by marked trees North... to the other forke thence down the said Swamp the several meanders to the Fork thence up the said Fork the several courses to the Beginning and 129 acres the residue is also bounded as followeth, to wit, Beginning at a stump on New Kent Road and Running thence South ... to two Lines (which) divide the said land from Doctor Carter's Land thence North ... to the aforesaid Road which said Line divides the said Land from the Land that Robert Lark now lives on thence down the several courses of the said Road to the Beginning.
5 March 1762.

Bk. 35, p. 552.

Thomas Hornsby, sunken ground or swamp land, 45 acres, Jas. City Co., bounded as followeth, to wit, Beginning at an Ash in a small branch that divides this from the land of the Hon. Philip Ludwell thence down the seven courses of the said Branch to the main Run of Pohaton Swamp at a corner thence up the several courses of the said Run to a corner ash on the South side of the Branch that divides this from the Land of Mr. Davis thence along the several courses of the said Hornsby's High Land as by the Patent there to the Beginning. 27 June 1764.

Commonwealth's Grants. The abstracts will be much shorter since the dates are Revolution and later period material. All are of Jas. City Co.

#8, p. 435, Warrant #21,836 & Issued 24 Dec. 1783. Joseph Crawley 637 3/4 acres, survey 20 Aug. 1785, parish of Jas. City; 187 3/4 acres being formerly patented the residue never before granted. Bounded between Crawley's and William Lee and running along a swamp, etc., thence leaving the large swamp called Pahatan Swamp and running up a small swamp, etc., thence leaving the swamp, etc., and running along a line of marked trees between the said Crowley and William Lee to the first; 8 Feb. 1787.

Bk. 9, p. 610, Warrant #21,836, issued 24 Dec. 1783, to John Cooper assignee of David Anderson, 413 acres by survey, 20 March 1786, parish of Blisland. Bounded at an alnut at the side of the marsh on the line between the said Cooper and James Pride, running across the Creek to a point of marsh on the other side South, thence down the Creek to the main creek & down it to the marsh thence down it, thence leaving the main Creek and running up the Creek which makes the Island at Low water mark, etc., to the lower dam and to the land thence running up the creek at low water mark the same course as before, etc., thence crossing the creek to a gut and up it to the head, thence up the Slash, thence up the left Branch, to a deep bottom run thence sown the water course; leaving the swamp and running North, etc., to the Beginning. 10 July 1787. (This is a long patent.)

Bk. 9, p. 613, Warrant #21,836, issued 24 Dec. 1783, to John Cooper assignee of David Anderson, 132 acres, Survey 20 June 1786, on the Chickahominy River, bounded at the Roaring hole on Old River and running up the said River on the Land Side North, to a bent, thence North, etc., thence crossing the river to the marsh and along it, etc., thence down the River to the lower part of Old River to the beginning. 6 July 1787.

Bk. 18, p. 105, Warrant #21,836, Issued 24 Dec. 1783, to Thomas Pate assignee of John Cooper who was assignee of David Anderson 89 3/4 acres, by Jury, 2 Sept. 1787, parish of Jas. City; bounded at Hay Stack point and running down the gutt to a Bent thence down it to the Creek, thence up the Creek, thence to Mount Porter thence running down along the sdie of the high Land belonging to the said Pate, thence to the beginning; 8 July 1788.

Bk. 18, p. 580, Warrant #21082, Issued 1 Dec. 1783, to John Blair as assignee of John Hopkins who was Assignee of David Anderson, 49 acres by Survey, 1 Dec. 1787, parish of Blisland (Blasland); bounded at the mouth of Millions gut on York river, running up the River to the mouth of Taskernash Creek thence up the said Creek to the fork in the Creek, then to the highland on the West fork thence down the side of the said Creek to the head of Metoons Gut thence down the gut to the beginning. 29 Oct. 1788.

Bk. 18, p. 588, to John Blair, October 24, 1788, 53 2/4 acres, the bound beginning at the mouth of a gut at Hankins landing on York River.

Bk. 19, p. 546, John Turner, July 30, 1789, 33½ acres, the bounds beginning at John Goodalls landing on John Coopers Mill Creek.

Bk. 20, p. 232, March 23, 1789, 76 acres, the bounds beginning at the Crossing place on Mount Swamp.

Bk. 22 (listed, but no entry.)

Bk. 25, p. 515, William Goodin, Feb. 7, 1792, 15 acres, Blisland Parish and the bounds beginning at a black (as in the Ms.) on Rockahock road, which divides the said Land (&) Richard Taylors.

Bk. 90, p. 769, John Wenchers, 24 Feb. 1840, 57:3:9 - no description.

Bk. 93, p. 27, Thomas Timberlake, 1 Aug. 1842, 109:1:18 & bounds beginning at a Sycamore at the fork of the Swamp to the West corner.

Bk. 122, J. R. Austin, 1 Aug. 1904, 175 acres, 32 po: at the junction of Gordon & Bush Neck Creek..

Appendix: A Problem of Sources.

From "Abstracts of the Proceedings of the Virginia Company of London," by Conway Robinson and Ed. by R. A. Brock 1889, Coll., Va. Hist. Soc., ii, 37.

By the Admiral and principal Governor of Virginia:
... I, Samuel Argall ... bounds and limits of Jamestown ... that is to say the whole island with part of the main land lying on the east side of Argall town, and adjoining upon the said island also the neck of land on the north part, and so to the further part of Archer's Hope; also Hog Island; and from thence to the four mile tree on the south, usually called by the name of Tappahannock, in all which several places of ground I hereby give license for the inhabitants of Jamestown to plant as members of the corporation and parish of the same ... 28 May 1619.

(From what office or source was this document taken? In "The Records of the Virginia Company of London, Ed. Susan M. Kingsbury, Vol. i, a list of Records is given, and the above is listed as #109, the source is given as Ms. Court Book, Va. Co., ii (no page is given), and pub. (1) Kingsbury, Rec. Va. Co., II (no page is given), Index; (2) Brock, Va. Co., II, 37.

It should be easy usually to check up the references given, and then use her work as an authority; it is without doubt a work of excellence. However, there are several considerations necessary to an understanding of reference material for the history of Jas. City Co. She intended to publish this document, but it does not appear in the text. I have searched the Mss. volumes of the source at the Library of Congress, and it is not there. It could have been in the section of the above date, or it could have been in the section when the Virginia Company was hearing the case of Gov. Argall. She printed everything in the Mss. carefully, so the obvious conclusion is that this document did not appear in the specified source when she was preparing the volumes for publication.

In his "First Republic," by Alexander Brown, p. 287, it is also published. He gives no source from which he obtained it.

In the Brock Ed. of the Va. Co., II, p. 30, the Court is dated 15 Dec. 1619, and the Va. Co. hearing of the Argall case is in progress. For several pages to follow there seems to be an excursus about Gov. Argall, using notes and documents not in the Randolph Mss., at this definite point, or not there at all. The material used is several years old, since the last date of the Randolph Court material used was 4 Dec. 1622 and the excursus ends on p. 48, Court a week after 4 Dec. 1622. The nearest guess from this publication as to the place of the source is the Library of Congress.

I have searched for this source in the Library of Congress, not only in the Ms. Div., but also in the Rare Book Room; I have also searched the Randolph Mss. at the Va. Hist. Soc., as well as the remains of both the Author and the Editor deposited in the Library of the Va. Hist. Soc., but with negative results. As far as I can discover, it is not in the Va. State Lib.

An indirect result of the realization that the source of this document may not be known, or even extent, is that the two sources of publication become much more valuable. There remain available copies of Brock's Va. Co., and fortunately there are many copies owned by libraries.)

Appendix II: Land Patents, Bk. I, pp. 3 & 4
See "Cavaliers and Pioneers," by Nell Marion Nugent, p. 2, her note concerning the missing pages 3 & 4. See Macalester College, Contributions, Ser. I, Appendix, pp. 32-3, Patent of George Yeardley in full; pp. 33-34, Patent to Ralph Hamor (in error, it is ascribed to Ralph Warner), in full.

By: Karon Mac Smith, Nixon, Texas

Adams, William 77
Adderson, Roger 53
Aesupp/Alsupp, James 8, 9, 12, 15, 39, 57
Alcock, ___ 53
Alesbury, Eliz 38
Alestres, ___ 44
Allam, John 52
   Julian 39
Allen, Gabriel 59
   John 42, 44
   Patience 12
   Robert 42
   Sam 68
Allingsworth, John 38
Allosser, Edw 41
Ally, Susan 65
Ambler, Edward 31, 32, 33, 34, 25
   Jacquelin 33, 34, 35
   John 28, 32, 33, 34, 35, 36
   Mary 35
   Molly 34
   Rebecca 34, 35
   Richard 26, 27, 28, 29, 30, 31, 33, 34
   Sally 34
Amory, Jno 44
Anbell, Tho 51
Anderson, Bartlett 29, 30
   David 29, 30, 83
   Derrick 75
   Frances 29, 30
   Robert 29, 30
Andrews, Robert 36
Andros, Sir Edmond 13, 14, 15, 17, 19, 65, 68, 69
Annwood, Roger 70
Anterbus(?), Mary 19
Archer, Mich 27
Argall, Samuel 85
Arminger, William 81
Arnold, John 63
   Thomas 13
Ash, ___ 62
   Lawrence 54
Ashbyfoot, John 38
Ashers, Robt 9, 11
Ashurst, Robert 27, 79
Athaway, Edward 33
Atkinson, Tho 75, 78
Austin, J. R. 84
Awborne, Rich 6
Ayleth, Wm. 19
Ayton, John 40, 41, 45, 46, 59, 60, 64, 65

Bacon, Eliz. 4, 5
   Nathaniel 4, 5, 12, 14, 15, 23, 38, 52, 57, 59, 64
Bailey/Bayley, ___ 61
   Geo. 41
   Wm. 20, 60
Bair/Baird, ___ 15, 22
   John 23, 25
   Margaret 25
Baker, Law 51
   Rachell 64
Baldwin/Bauldwin, John 3, 10, 15, 18, 48, 66
   Nich 44
Ball, Richard 73
Ballard, Mr. 76
Ballow, Charles 25, 26
Barber, Anne 41
   John 6, 15, 23, 40
   Lettice 9
Barker, ___ 44
   George 79
Barloe, Jno 67
Barnet, Nicho 53
Barn(e)house, Richard 39, 42

Bareatt/Barrett, Catherine 76, 77
   Edith 76
   James 62, 76, 77
   Margaret 53
   Wm. 62, 70, 76, 77
Barron, Andr. 67
Bash, John 74
Bassel, Ralph 50
Bassett, ___ 56
   Tho 38
Bateman, Mathew 18
Batts, Mr. 42
Baugh, Wm 5
Baxter, Jane 52
Baylor, John 33
Beach, Judith 52
Bear, Wm 76
Beardwell, Rich 39
Bedford, Wemih(?) 42
   Wm. 40
Bee, Ralph 17
Beebs, Rebecca 70
   Wm. 70
Bell, John 53
   Rich'd. 38
   Wm. 44
Bellini, Charles 36
Belomy/Bellomy, Jabe 9
   Job 80
Benjamin (See Eggeston)
Bennet(t), Catherine (or C. Tenent) 71
   Richard 38, 55, 56
Benough, Ja 21
Berkeley, J. 25
   Dame Frances 46
   Sir William 3, 4, 6, 7, 8, 37, 38, 40, 41, 42, 43, 54, 61
Bernard, Capt. 38
Betterly, Fran 69
Beverley, Robert 5, 13, 14, 15, 16, 19, 20, 21, 26, 29, 67
Beyforth, Joseph 18
Bishop, Mr. 46, 53
Blacks:
   Abel 34
   America 34
   Amy 64
   Ben 34
   Betty 65
   Billy 34
   Booby 68
   Boss 65
   Claye 63
   Crocky 65
   Cupid 33
   Daniel 65
   Dick 58
   Emanell Cambrew 40
   Frank 65
   Genny 34
   George 33(2)
   Geo. Row Mingol 44
   Grace 33(2)
   Guy 33, 63
   Hannah 34
   Hector 63
   Jack 58, 65
   Jerry 34
   John 33
   Jorny 65
   Judith 65
   La. Nicholls 62
   Little Edith 34
   Mariah 63
   Mark 33
   Marreah 65
   Moll Cook 33
   Ned 22, 33, 34
   Nero 64

Blacks, Cont.
   Old Ben 33
   Old Edith 33, 34
   Peg 34
   Polly 34
   Pompy 63
   Prancer 62
   Puy Chambo 62
   Sam 69
   Sawney 34
   Sharper 34
   Sue 63
   Tamo 34
   Tom 58
   Tony 65, 68
   Venis 33
   Will 34, 63, 69
   Wm. Leverpool 28
Blackley, Eliz 42
Blaikley, Mr. 73, 74, 75
Blair (See Bair/Baird)
   James 16, 57, 81
   John 83
Bland, ___ (Randolph) 22
   Ed 53
   Richard 25
Blewet, Mr. 62
   Ann 62
Bobby, Thomas 9, 47, 50, 58, 59, 63, 64
Bolling, Robert 26
Bolt, Roger 64
Bone, Josias 76
Bororye, Thomas 54
Bouth, Thos 24
Bowman, John 43
Bowry, Thomas 49
Bowser, Hen 51
Boys, Samuel 81
Bracket, Elizabeth 66
   Mark 66
Bradford, ___ 56
Bradly, Hannah 62
   Robert 62
Branin, Wm. 47
Bray, Col. 82
   Esq. 49
   Angelica 68
   David 71, 72
   James 39, 65
Brent, George 14
Brereton, Thos. 4, 37
Brewer, Edmond 63
   Sackville 69, 76, 77
Bridges, Thos. 39
Brisco(e), Wm. 9, 11, 15, 16, 36
Brisse, Matt 53
Bristow, Thos 38
Broadhurst, Andrew 58
Broadnax, Anne 26, 27
   Wm 15, 17, 26, 27, 29
Broadribb/Broadribley, Mr. 61, 67, 68
   Abra 20
   Benjamin 20, 21, 28
   Lydia 20, 21
   Susan 21
   Thomas 20, 21, 28
   Wm. 20, 21, 22, 60, 63, 67
Brocas, Capt. 38
   Wm. 3, 37
Bromfield/Brumfield, Mr. 53, 60, 62, 63, 67
   Law 47
Brookhouse, Thomas 10
Brook(e)s, Rich 64
   Walter 52
Brown/Browne, Henry 4, 37
   John 13
   Tho. 63
   Will. 39, 48

Browning, Humpherey 53
  John 42
Bryan, Benjamin 28
Buberry, Jno 62
Bucher, Joseph 64
Buck, Tho 47
Bugden, Alex 42
Bullivant, Francis 14, 15, 19, 26, 29
Burdett, Sarah 45
Burnell/Burnett, Mr. 41, 45, 46, 49
Burney, Mary (als Dormer) 53
Burton, Hatcher(?) 30
  Ralph 50
Burwell, Mr. 60, 65
  John 32
  Katherine Cacon 81
  Nath 21
Bush, John 5, 75
  Jos 39, 75
  Nich 39, 47, 48, 75
Bushton, Bryan 38
Butler, Wm. 52
Butt(s), John 64
  Stephen 51
Buxton, Robt. 38
Byrd, Wm. 33, 35, 77, 80
Cannon, Robt. 49
Capwell, Tho. 65
Car(e)y, Henry Jr. 25
  Miles 39, 42
  Wilson-Miles 32
Carpenter, John 42
Carrell (See Darrell), Benj. 39
Carron, Ed. 73, 74
Carter, Dr. 82
  Charles 21
  Edward 4
  John 21, 38
  Robert 21
Caryl, Ben. 52
  Eliz 52
  Hen 52
Cassick, John 52
Catt (See Coates)
Causye, ___ 38
Champion, Wm. 50
Chancy, Gilbert 56
Chandler, Francis 41
  Jno 67
Charles, Phillip 43, 69
  Tho 59
Charlton, Edw'd 32
Chemerson/Chermision, Joseph 22
Cherineson, Dr. 80
Chesleigh/Chudleigh, ___ 5
  Ann 16, 17, 18, 19, 66
  James 15, 17, 18, 66, 69
Chesley, Dan 59
  Phillip 41
Chessman, Wm. 58
Chicheley, Henry 10
Chidman (See Shipdan)
Chiles, Mr. 6, 37
  Susan (na) 9, 44, 50
  Walter 3, 5, 6, 8, 39, 44
Chilton, Edward 3, 4, 52, 53, 60, 65
Chiswell, Cha 22
Choil, Wm. 67
Claiborn/Claybourn, Wm., Jr. 8, 16, 28, 30, 38
  Wm. 68
Clark(e) (See Clerke), Ben 35
  Eliza 64
  Hump 41
  John 61
  Richard 8
  Robert 61
  Wm 78
Cla(y)ton, John 23, 27

Cla(y)ton, Cont.
  Tho 7, 9
Clerke (see Clarke), Wm. 51
Clipon, Edward 78
Coates, Isaac 46, 53
  John 63
Cobham, Augustine 54, 56
Cock/Cocke, James 22
  Richd 21
  Thos 22
  Stephen 64
Cocket(t), James 37, 42
Cogin, Tho T. 39
Cole, Edward 77 (probably Cowles)
  John 38
  John F. 39
  Robert 25
  Thomas 25
  Wm. 9, 11, 13, 28
Coleburn, Wm. 72
Coleby, Andrew 62
Coleman, Mr. 37
  Anthony 22
Colgil, Wm. 76
Collins, Mr. 49, 65
  James 64
  Matthew 65
Comens, Antho 67
Comris/Couris, Wm. 80
Coney, Tho. 60
Congers, Jno 47
Conoway, Robt. 10
Cooper, John 83
Copeland, Joseph
Corbin/Corbyn, Anth. 60
  Brice 60
  Hen 38
Cowch, Lawrence 44
Cowles, Mr. 56, 63, 74
  Capt. 77
  Edward 43, 72, 73, 74, 77
  Thos. 72, 73, 74, 77
Coyt, Wm. 53
Crafford/Crawford, David 39, 40, 56, 78
Craw, Peter 70
Crawl(e)y, Joseph 83
  Nath 25
  Robert 55
Crisam, Jno 44
Crosse, Math 45
Crump, Eliza 43
  John 43, 50
Culpeper, Alexander 14
  Marguerite 14, 21
Custis, John 12, 57
Cutler, Jno 62
Cutts, Susan 44

Dale, Robt. 51
Dall, W. 12
Damon, Joanna 70
Danber/Dauber, Nich 38
Dance/Dancy, Mr. 50
  Francis 56
  John 38
  Stephen 72
Dangerfield, Wm. 32
Darrell (See Carrell), Benjamin 39
Davenport, Joseph 14
Daveys/Davies, ___ 63
  Robt. 47
  Wm. 68
Davis, ___ 55, 83
  John 33
  Kath 62
  Moses 56
  Robert 67
  Wm 19, 40, 62
Davison, David 72, 73
Daw(e)s, Fra 50

Daw(e)s, Cont.
  Joseph 19
Dawson, Wm. 31
Day, Tho. 60
Dean(e), John 9, 39, 50
Decket/Deckit, Thomas 16
Dees, Emanuell 21, 68
Denkins, Thomas 73
Dennis, Richard 23
Dewe, Thomas 4
Dickenson, Griffin 54
Digg(e)s, Esq. 48, 55
  Edward 3
Dilliard, James 82
Dobonias, John 39
Doby, ___ 54, 55
  John 51
Doran, John 81
Dormer, John 53, 55
  Mary 53
  Rebecca 55
  Wm. 44, 55
Downes, Wm. 59
Dowtin, Antho 17
Doyley, Cope 19
Drecoit/Drewit, Wm. 43
Drummond, Mr. 33, 37
  Wm. 9, 13, 21, 23, 31, 43, 44
Drysdale, Hugh 80
Dubosse, Wm. 42
Dudley, William 32
Duke, ___ 81
  Capt. 49, 56
  Col. 76
  Hen 49, 57, 60, 64, 65, 71
  James 75
  John 44
  Mary 49
Dunahon, Cath 65
Dunnham, Hen 52
Duval, Mr. 36

Eallon, Jno 45
Ebberle, Thomas 74
Ebonyman, Alex 19
Edloe, ___ 44
  John 51
  Mathew 4, 44
Edmonds, ___ 75
Edwards, Ambrose 58
  John 38
  W. 59
  Wm. 7, 12, 15, 16, 17, 18, 19, 37, 57, 59, 60, 65, 69
Eggleston, Mr. 22
  Ben 9, 11, 21, 60, 67, 68, 69
Elcome/Elsome, Wm. 41, 45, 46, 57, 59, 65
Eldridge, Sam. 51
  T. 23
  Tho. 24
Ellerby, Edward 51
Elleston, Edward 64
Ellibris, ___ 51
Ellis, William 81
Elliot, Jno. 75
Elock, John 56
Elsmore, Jno 58
Elwood, John 6
England, Humphrey 47, 58
Epes, Francis 5
Esterwether, Rich 4
Etherall, Tho 38
Evans, Owen 42
Everard, Thos. 35
Everett, John 17

Fairfax, ___ (Lord?) 14
  Catherine 14, 21

Fairfax, Cont.
  Thomas, Lord F. 21
Falk, Jane 66
  Thomas 66
Farmer, Beirobe 62
Farrar/Ferrar(s), John 37
  Robt. 44
  Wm. 3, 5
Farrell, Hubert 44
Felgate, John 41
Fellones, Edward 42
Field, Theophilus 26
Finne, Alexander 82
  Wm. 24
Fish, ___ 67
Fitchett, John 18, 22, 66
Fitzhugh, Wm. 14
Forbody, Charles 41
Ford, Christopher, Jr. 28
Foreman, ___ 51
Forrester, William 21
Fowler, Barth 69
Fowles, Wm. 38
Frayser, Wm. 25
Freeman, Capt. 37
  Mr. 54, 55
  George 71, 72
  Phillip 45
Fry, ___ 58
  Joseph 53, 57, 58, 59
  Wm. 47, 51, 57, 58, 59
Fulcher, John 10, 14, 15, 18, 48, 66
Fysher, John 68
Fustain, Ralph 79
Fyps (See Phipps)

Gammon, Jno 44
Gardner, Martin 9, 10, 11
  Tho 6
Garland, John 29, 30
Gaskine, Apel 53
Gauler, Henry 53
George II 26
George III 32
Gibbs, William 34
Gibbons, John 33
Gibson, Peter 52
Gilbert, Edith 76
  Henry 76, 77
Gill, George 9
Gilles, Edw. 46
Gilly/Gylly, ___ 73
  Edward 44, 73
  John 38
Glanlin, Jno 45
Glazbrook, Richard 82
Glenister, Peter 53
Godian, ___ 55
  Andrew 56
Goddin/Goding, Isaac 82
Goldsmith, Wm. 53
Gon, Joanna 59
Gooch, Wm. 27, 28, 30, 31, 80
Goodale, John 73, 83
  Nicholas 69
Goodin, Wm. 84
Goodrich, Benjamin 79
  Robert 75, 79
Gooseby, Martha 34
Goosley, Cary 34
  Will 34
Goram, John 64
Gordon, Samuel 26
Goslin, Jno 62
Goss, Charles 50
  Eddy 50
Gouge, Ralph 3
Goulby/Gouldsby, Thomas 72, 74
Go(w)en, Mihil 78
Gowree, Mihil 42
Grace, Mr. 38

Graves, Richd. 34
  Tho 66
Green(e), Anne 26
  Charles 40
  Edward 77
  Gerard 41
  John 26, 29, 63
  Thomas 80
Gregg, Thos. 21
Grice (See Grise), ___ 78
Griffin, Geo 53
  Rice 53
  Tho 56
Griffith, Edward 45
  Robert 49
Grinfeild, John 55
Grise (See Grice), ___ 55
Grimes (See Grymes), ___ 49
Grocer, Eliz 62
Grubury, John 39
Grymes (See Grimes), Tho. 41
Gunnell, Edward 42
Gwin, ___ 56

Haidon/Haydon, Clement 55
Haines, Jno 69
  Robert 38
Hair, Jno 63
Hal(e)y, ___ 59
  James 54, 76
  John 44
Hall, John 11
  Mathew 25
  Wm. 69
Ham, Mr. 49
  Jerry 53
Hammond, M. 37
Hamor, Ralph 85
Hampton, Thomas 49
Hancock, John 52
  Thomas 65
Hankin, ___ 83
Hannot, Sarah 66
Harby, George 55
Hardin, Wm. 51
Harmer, Amb 3
Harris, ___ 35
  James 56
  John 16, 17, 31, 33
  Robert 47
  Wm. 22
Harrison, Edw. 9, 11
  Eliz. 35
  Geo. 70
  Wm. 7
Hartwell, Henry 6, 8, 9, 12, 13, 15, 16,. 18, 23, 36, 46, 47, 50, 57, 60, 65, 66, 69
  Jane 16
Harvey, John 3
Harwood, Mary 32
  William 32
Haskin, Edw'd. 67
Haveat, Wm. 51
Hawby, John 74
Hawly, Wm. 49
Hawthorne, Philip 10
Hayman, Jno 39
Hearne, Wm. 44
Heart, James 28
Heathrosh, Henry 76
Henley, Turner 32
Henshawe, ___ 63
Herd, ___ 82
Heyman, Peter 14
Heyne, Fra 49
Hichman/Hitchman (See Hitchcock)
  Wm. 40, 41, 45
Hicks/Hix, John 49, 53, 65
Higby, Edw. 38
Higginson, Mrs. 47
  Hump 37

Higginson, Cont.
  Ro 28
  Robert 34
  Wm. 53
Hill(s), Edward 3, 13, 37, 42
  Eliz 3
  Richard 70
  Rose 53
  Thomas 3
  Wm. 52
Hilliard, Thomas 81
Hinchin, Edw'd. 60
Hind, ___ 74
Hingham, E. 11, 12
Hinich, Jno 62
Hint, ___ 74
Hinton (See Winton), ___ 55
Hitchceiks/Hitchcock, ___ 16, 51
  John 73
  Wm. 46
Hobbs, Maj. 40
Hobert (See Roberts), Rich'd 73
Hodge, Richard 11
Hoe, Petre(?) 76
  Rice 42, 51, 61, 76
Holden/Holder, ___ 12
  Anne 11, 12, 15, 18, 20, 36
  Richard 6, 15, 17, 23, 39, 44, 69
  Robert 45
Holli(i)day/Holyday, ___ 23
  Mr. 50
  Hana 9
  Thomas 9, 11, 15, 16, 36
Holloway, John 77
Holmes, Hugh 36
Holt, Maj. 6
  Col. 46
  Adam 58
  Robert 41, 75
  Thomas 28
  William 34
Homins, Wm. 7
Hone, Theophilus 4, 8
  Theo Jr. 45, 46
  Thomas 45, 46
Hood, James 62, 67
Hooker (See Hooper), ___ 79
  Edward 52, 70
  Will 6, 8
Hooper (See Hooker), John 4
  Thomas 21
Hopkins, ___ 55
  John 14, 19, 21, 83
Hornsby, Thomas 82, 83
Horton, Wm. 60
Hoskins, Jno 46
Howard, John 14, 15, 19, 23 26, 28, 59, 64
Hoy, Eliz. 80
  John 80
Hubbard/Huberd (See Hubbert), James 11
  Mathew 61
  Robert 78
Hubbert/Hubert, Jno 59
  Robert 44, 61, 78
Huby, Tho 62
Huck, Edward 47
Hudson, Kath 42
Hughes, Ann 19
  George 19, 38
Humberk, Richard 76
Hunt, Mr. 54
  George 59, 78
  Tho. 39
  Wm. 51, 52, 61, 63, 72, 77
Hupey, Anne 60
Hyde, Anne 81

Hyde, Cont.
  Rebecca 81

Indwell, Philip 74
Ingerton, Jno 57
Ingles, Mongo 25

Jaceson, Will 38
Jackson, Christopher 27, 77, 78, 79
Ja(c)quelin, Edward 21, 25, 26, 27, 28, 29
  Martha 33 (See Phillips)
James, Mr. 3, 5, 36
  Martin 12
  Rice 41
  Rachel 6
  Richard 6, 8, 10, 13, 18, 19, 23, 39, 48, 59, 66
Jane(?), John 16
Janett, Eliza 58
Jarrett, Eliz 18
  Johannah 18, 19
  John 13, 15, 18, 19, 20, 27
  Mary 18
Jefferys, Sir Jeffery 18, 19, 21
  Simon 23, 30, 31, 71, 73, 74, 76
Jenifer, Dan'l 13
Jenings/Jennings, Edmond/Edmund 12, 20, 22, 25, 27, 28, 69, 70, 79, 80, 81
  Francis 12, 13
  James 77, 78
  Robert 20
Jenkins, Henry 13, 18, 19, 21
Jennett, Elizabeth 62
Jerdon, Francis 34
Jessell, James 19
Johnson, Anthony 43
  Garrett 47
  John 50, 63
  Peter 40
  Wm. 53
Jones, ___ 53, 54
  Anne 41
  Burnell 82
  Diana 60
  Eliz. 47
  Frederick 71
  Harwood 32
  Hester 54
  John 66
  Joshua 82
  Richard 62*
  Robert 38
  Thomas 78
Jordan, Col. 36
  Saml. 35
Jubille, Dorothy 19
Jues(?), Wm. 58
Kean, Lt. Col. Tho. 5
Keeney, Ellinor 62
Kemp(e), Mathew 47
  Richard 3, 8, 37, 38
Kent, Wm. 62
Keser, Anne 62
Kingsmill, Eliz 4, 5
  Richard 4, 5
Kinsey, John 52
  Paul 52
Kinson(?), Jn. 21
Kirkman, Francis 37, 38, 39, 45
Knight, Mr. 47
  John 47
  Joseph 75
Knipe, Barth 46
Knowles, Betheia 5
  John 4, 5, 6, 9, 10, 18, 36, 48, 66
  Wm. 56

Lacy, David 56
La Force, Rene 24
Lamb, Will. 38
Lambeth, ___ 79
Land, Curtis 53
Lande, Timothy 69
Landerson, Wm. 40
Langley, Eliz 47
Lark, Robert 82
Lashell, Perian 73
Lawrence, ___ 14, 52, 67
  Rich 41
Lee, George 11
  Richard 4, 13, 52
  Thomas 74
  William 83
Leech, Robert 58
Lendoll, Wm. 56
Lever, Jno 60, 64
Lewis, ___ 55
  Mr. 19
  Marg. 45
Lide, Ro 13
Lidwell (See Ludwell)
Liell, Daniel 43
Light, Jno 41
Lightfoot, Mr. 74
  Fras 24
  Philip 24, 68, 69
  John 20, 69, 70, 71
  W. 22
Ligon, Tho 41
Littler, ___ 70
  Jno 39
Loe, Geo 13
Loften/Lofftine, ___ 62, 63
  Cornelius 53
London, Thos. 45
Long, Peter 46
Loo, Clement 62
Loveing, Anne 40
  Tho. 40
Ludlow, Mr. 38
Ludwell, Col. 20
  Mr. 38
  Philip 6, 17, 21, 23, 24, 27, 28, 52, 64, 67, 68, 69, 71, 72, 79, 80, 81, 82
  Thomas 6, 37, 38, 39, 42
Lund, Tho 52
Lynns, Roger 38

McGill, Charles 36
Macklin, William 77
Madison, James 36
Major, John 67
Mallard, Tho 38
Mandy, Arthur 46
Mank, Stapleton 12
Mamin/Manning, William 65
Maples, Thomas 40, 45, 46
Marable(s), Capt. 21, 69
  Benj. 30, 31
  Eliz. 80
  George 9, 14, 17, 18, 19, 22, 23, 30, 31, 39, 69
  Mary 17
  Wm. 27, 76, 79, 80
Markland, Isabella 67
Marlin, Robt. 52
Marsten/Marston, Mr. 61
  Eliz 57
  John(Son?) 34, 57
  Thomas 61
Mason, ___ 56
  James 46
  Tho. 38
Matherod, Henry 76
Mathew(s), Jeremiah 54
  Sam'll 37
Maybey, Brice 60
Mayden, Henry 46

May(es), Wm. 5, 6, 8, 11, 12, 15, 28, 39, 40, 57
Meekins, Thomas 53
Menefy, Geo 3
Meredith, Thos. 45
Meriwether/Merryweather, Fra. 16, 17, 57
  Nicholas 4, 5, 10, 11, 12
Merriman/Merryman, Jo. 39
  John 47, 69
Messenger, Hercules 53
Michell/Michaell, Tho 64
  Wm. 44
Middleton, Thomas 21
Miles, Jorie(?) 46
Miller, Hugh 26
Mills, Hannah 35
Milton, Tho 9, 11, 39
Mitchel, Tho. 52
Molsworth, Guy 4
Moreland, Anne 78
  Francis 78
Moor(e)/More, David 9
  John 28
  Marg. 44
  Tho. 46
Morgan, Mr. 69
  Robert 67
  Wm. 42, 67
Morley, Margaret 49
Morris, Benja 32
  Sarah 46
  William 29
Morrison, Francis 4, 5, 22, 37, 38
Morse, Geo 47
Morton, John 22, 25
Mosely, Morris 49
Moyle, Wm. 45
Moyse(s), Nicholas 74, 75, 76
  Richard 73
Murray, William 78
Musson, Hen. 42
Muttlow, Peter 30
Myer, Eliz 18
  Wm. 18

Nance, ___ 63
  William 62
Nesham, Thomas 68, 72
Newell/Nowell, ___ 23, 57
  Capt. 75
  Mrs. 51
  David 8, 9, 10, 18, 44, 48, 60, 66, 67
  Jonathan 4, 6, 8, 9, 10, 11, 18, 48, 66
  Lydia 47, 51, 57, 58, 59, 63
Newman, Nath 60
New, Richard 48
Nicholas, Mr. 36
  Anne 32
  George 35
  Lewis 35
  Robert Carter 32, 33, 35
Nicholson, Francis 13, 20, 69, 70
Noell (See Newell)
North, Tho 47
Norton, George 35
  George F. 36
  John Hatley 36
Norvell, Wm. 31
Norwell, Capt. 74
Nott, Edw. 70
Nugent, William 30

Oatby, Fra 41
Oatly, Dorcey 68
Obey, Anthony 53
Oglevy, James 64

Okey, Traga 41
Omoonees, ___ 16, 36
  James 17
Overman, ___ 70

Pacamon, John 44
Pack, Graves 78
Page, ___ 11, 21, 33
  John 8, 11, 16, 18, 53, 56, 57, 66
  Robert 36
Pagg(s), Mathew 42, 43
Paine/Payne, Rich'd 52
  Wm. 41
Pall, Thomas 38
Parchmore(?), ___ 40
Parish, Joseph 78
Park(e), Dan'l. 68
Parker, Robt. 52
  Tho. 58
Parkins/Perkins, Mrs. 37, 48
  Christopher 26, 28, 29, 33
  Eliz. 4, 28, 29
  Jane 70
  Thomas 4
Partich, Leo 38
Pate, Thomas 83
Pattison, Kate 71
Paulett, Wm. 47
  Wm. I. 39
Peach, Dorothy 12
Peak, ___ 72
Peall, Rich'd 73
Pearson, Thomas 70
Peawde, William 49, 56
Peirce/Peirse (See Pierce),
  Fra 62
  Grace 62
  Richard 62
  Wm. 3
Pell, Timothy 51
Penn, William 11
Perry, Ellis 59
  Micajah 17, 18
Personn (or Porsonn), ___ 69
Pettit, Joseph 19
Pettiver, John 69
Pettus, Capt. 38, 47
  Tho 37
Phillip(s), ___ 52, 54, 59
  David 58, 59
  Hannah Jaquelin 33
  Richard 75
Phipps/Fipps/Fyps, John 4, 5, 6, 10, 17, 22, 25, 48, 68
  Mary 4, 25
Pichetts/Picketts, Benjamin 27, 70, 79
  Ell 52
Pierce (See Peirce), Wm. 38
Piggot(t), Spencer 9, 11, 12
Pinhorne/Pimhorne, John 6, 40
Pintt, Wm. 73
Pleasants/Pleasents, John 15
  Joseph 25, 26
Poires, Wm. 8
Polin, James 62
Pollard, James 66
Pond, Margaret (als Morley) 49
  Samuel 49
Poor, Anne 47
Poray, David 72
Porter, Daniel 81, 82
Porteus, Robert 79
Porteridge, Roger 5
Posse, Wm. 52
Potter, ___ 53
Powell, Alfred 36
  Ed. 73, 74
  Tho. 67
Preston, Joseph 49
Prickinson (See Dickenson/
  Wilkinson), Griffin 52

Pride, James 83
Prior/Pryor, Nich. 47, 62
Proctor, Stephen 9, 10
  Winifred 10, 11
Prosan(?), ___ 55
Prosser, Tho. 35
Pruers, ___ 62
Purdey, Rich. 38
Pussan, William 21
Pyle, Math. 62

Rabley/Radley, ___ 16
  Eliz 36
  Thomas 9, 12, 17, 23, 37, 57, 69
Ramball/Ramble, ___ 61
Rams(e)y, Capt. 40
  Edw. 39
Randall, John 62
Randolph, ___ 26
  Col. 20
  Mr. 30
  Edward 22
  Edm'd 35
  Henry 4, 6, 22, 23, 24, 37, 38, 39, 61
  Isham 22, 24
  John 22, 24
  Mary 22
  Peter 81
  Richard 22, 24, 25
  Thomas 12, 22, 23, 24, 26, 35
  Wm. 12, 15, 22, 23, 24, 25, 26
Raven, Dan'l 67
Reade, Geo. 59
  Gwyn 33
Reador, And. R. 39
Redman, Robt. 62
Reekes/Ricks/Rix, Mrs. 3
  Eliz 4, 5
  John 4, 6
  Richard 4, 5, 10
Reene, Thos. 52
Remble, Sam 74
Rennffee, Nicholas 75
Reuthen, Joseph 63
Reynolds, John 51
  Wm. 53
Rice, Wm. 53
Richardson, Hen. 64
Ridley, Edward 78
  Peter 78
Rigby, Robt. 52
Roberts, Hen. 50
  John 57
  Richard (See Hobert) 74
  Sarah 58
Robertson, Na. 17
  Wil. 22, 23, 25
Robins, Obed. 4
Robinson, Henry 30
  John 62
Rogers, Mr. 73
  Henry 76
  Thomas 71
Rolfe, Thomas 48, 81
Rooke, Bryan 43
Roos, Tho. 69
Roscow, Wm. 16
Rosse, Edward 14, 15, 17, 27, 28, 68
  John 51
Royall, Jos Jr. 24
Ruhn(?), John Jr. 32
Rumbal, ___ 74
Russell, Samuel 70

Sacke, M. 11
Sadler, Tho. 46
Sanders, Francis 42
  George 49

Sanderson, Cont.
  Robert 31
Sanderson, Mr. 52
  Edward 4, 9, 23, 41, 42
Sanghorne, Will 34
Sareazin, Step 25
Sarsnett/Sarsuett (See
  Susnett), Will 6, 40
Scarburgh, Edmond 41
Schofeild, Alex 62
Sclater, John 25
Scorey, Will'm (Guil?) 9, 10
Scott, Thomas 42
Seajam, John 64
Sedwick, I. 12
Seimer, Jno. 50
Selden, Rich. 38
Seniro, John 37
Shaddock (See Studdick),
  Henry 73, 74
She___, Wm. 11
Shell, John 54, 73
Shepherd, Eliz. 61
Sherman, Michael 14
  William 70
Sherwood, ___ 12
  Mr. 57
  Rachell 18, 19
  Tho. 7
  Wm. 7, 8, 9, 10, 11, 12, 13, 14, 15, 16, 17, 18, 19, 20, 21, 31, 33, 36, 48, 59, 66
Shesard, Tho. 58
Shilling, Wm. 62
Shipdam, Edmond 4, 5
  Eliz. 4, 5
Shnibb, Samuel 22
Shoar, Robt. R. 39
Short, Mary 70
Shydman (See Shipdam)
Side, Robert 73
Sisan, Col. 15
Sisly, Appia 68
Skips, Eliza 64
Slane, Ambrose 9
Smallpage, Robert 57
Smith, ___ 33
  Chris 6, 22
  Fran 29, 30
  Capt. John 7
  John 31, 34, 50, 62(2), 79
  Lydia 22
  Maurice 52
  Philip 80
  Richard 62, 67
  Robert 38
  Roby 62
Snead, Robt. 62
Snow, Hen 53
Soan(e), Henry 58, 81
  John 11, 13, 16, 36, 53, 54, 56, 57, 61, 71, 73, 74, 77
  William 46
Soillman, John 64
Sorrell, Mr. 41, 45, 64
  Jno. 62
  Mary 66
  Martin 76
  Robert 65
Speed, John 75
Spencer, Nicholas 10, 11, 47
Spicer, Arthur 19
  R. 17
Spottswood, A. 71, 72, 79
Spratley, Eliz. 21
  John 21
Spring, Robert 9
Spruell, Godfrey 54
Stabbs, Rich'd 65
Stark, Wm. 26

Sta(u)nton, Anne 28
  Wm. 39
Stegg(s), Mr. 38
  Thomas 5, 38, 42
Stephens/Stevens, Wm. 38, 64
Steward, John 11
Stith/Styth, ___ (Randolph) 22
  John 23, 62, 63, 67
Stone, Thomas 38
Storey, Francis 60, 63, 67
Strahell, Jane 38
Stratles, James 54
Stratton, Lucy 52
Strong, Wm. 51, 63
Studdick (See Shaddock), Henry 73
Sumers, Mary 70
Susnett (See Sarsnett), Wm. 39
Swan(n), Col. 36
  Mary 47
  Rich 38
  Tho. 38, 39, 42, 73
Sweet, Tho. 53
Sydnor, Fortu 23, 24
Symons, Ruth 62

Taliaferro, Rich 31
Tarent, Leo 21
Taylo(u)r(s), Mary 59
  Richard 84
  Thomas 68
  Wm. 43, 53
  Zachary 10
Tennent (See Bennet)
Teton, Kath. 69
Thacker, C. C. 3, 10, 14, 19, 20, 70
Thelfeild, Sam'l 62
Thomas, Hester 51
  John 70
  Lazarus 19, 70
  Wm. 51, 55
Thomason, John 63
Thom(p)son, ___ 73, 78
  Charles 28
  David 64
  Henry 9, 65
  James Sr. 72
Thorp, Otho 25
Tialio, ___ 52
Timberlake, Thomas 84
Tinberell, Nath 62
Timson, Capt. 25
Timsley/Tinslie/Tinseley, ___ 53, 56
  Grace 62
  Thomas 43, 50
Titterbon, Robt. 51
Tolbutt, Capt. 19
Toping, Eliz. 36
  Joseph 36
Towner, Thomas 60
Townsend, Rich. 37
Trason, Mary 38
Travis, ___ 15, 18, 35, 63
  Mr. 49, 66
  Edward 25, 26, 33, 35, 50, 52
  Edward Champion 26, 29, 30, 81
Trayser, Wm. 22
Tree, ___ 3
Tucker, Jane 64
Tuftain/Tuftian/Tufton, Ralph 27
Tullett/Tullitt, John 21, 22, 27
Tully, Thomas 8
Turner, George 39
  James 58, 62
  John 39, 42, 55, 83
Turtle, Robt. 45
Tuskin, Ralph 19

Twade, Tho. 39
Tyler, Lyon G. 8, 12
Tyree, Richard 81

Underhill, John 9, 36
Usher, Lawrence 20

Vadin/Vodin, Isaac 55
  John 55
Vahan, Jone 47
Valentine, ___ 75
  Nicholas 74
Varny, James 47, 61
  Peter 39
Vere/Were, John 74
Vobe, Anne 82
Vordale, John 44
Vynall, Alice 38

Wadd, Jos. 44
Wadding, James 8
  Susanna 8
Wade, Mr. 46
  Edward 65
  John 58, 70
  Joseph 72, 81
  Mary 49
  Robt. 81
Wager, Wm. 21, 28
Waldron/Waldrum, Tho 62
Walker, Alexander 9, 39
Waller, Ben 16, 26, 27, 28, 31, 32, 34, 36
Walter(s), ___ 56
  Thomas 51, 54, 72
Walthor, Nath 28
Warberton/Warburton, ___ 55
  Allisand 34
  Thomas 47
  William 32, 34
Warden/Wardon, Thomas 47, 58
Wardey, Rich. 19
Warner, Augustine 4
  Ralph 85
Warradine, James 42
Watnye, Dam 52
Wat(t)son, ___ 74
  Isaac 39
  John 16, 25, 26, 52, 73, 78
  Joseph 22
  William 55
Watts, Mary 41
Waugh, John 18
Webb, ___ 36, 51, 54, 56
  Giles 20
  Wm. 48
Webber, Tho 42
Webster, Richard 4, 10, 48
Welberry, Rich 38
Welbourne, Thomas 13
Welch, James 62
  Edward 65
Weldon, Poynes 14
  Sam 57
Wellman, Antho. 67
Wells, Gregory 43, 62, 63
  Thomas 69
Wenchers, John 84
Were (See Vere)
West, John 3, 37, 38
Wetherall, ___ 54
  Robert 37, 38
Whaley, James 19
  Mary 25, 27
Wheateby, Jno. 58
Whis(?), Mathew 75
Whitby, John 30
White, Col. 10, 49
  Maj. 23
  John 12, 43
  Phill 44
  W. 12
  Wm. 8, 11, 24, 25, 39, 57
Whitehead, Charles 70

Whitehead, Cont.
  Nazareth 70
Whiteing, Henry 13
Whittacar/acre/Whittaker,
  Richard 40
  Wm. 39, 40, 47, 71, 78
Wigg, Wm. 57
Wilby, John 49
Wilkins, ___ 67
  John 11
  Wm. 76
Wilki(n)son, (See Prickinson), ___ 35
  Edward 28, 34
  John 44
  Thomas 52, 68
Williams, ___ 58, 61
  George 19
  Isaac 63
  John 38, 50, 59, 63
  Mathew 69
  Nicho 53
  Richard 50, 58, 61, 63, 64
  Ruth 67
  Xian 38
Williamson, Jno. 50
Willis, James 64
Wilson, Willy 16
Wincoff, Robert 38
Windet, Edw'd 53
Winston (See Winton), Wm. 56
Winter, ___ 55
  Richard 9
Winton (See Hinton), ___ 66
Wolfe, ___ 51, 54
Womsley, ___ 56
  Roger 73
Wood, ___ 55
  Abraham 4, 38
  H. 26
  Sibella 62
  Tho. 53
  Wm. 59
Woodbone, Mary 63
Woodhouse, Thomas 6, 18, 40, 66
Woodson, John 22
Woodwarth, ___ 75
Woodward, George 45
  John 74
  Wm. 20, 27, 70
Worington, Tho. 39
Workman, Daniel 70
  Mary 70
Wormenel, Tho. 53
Wormeley/Wormley, Sec'y 15
  Christopher 13, 59, 60
  Ralph 13, 14, 18
  Wm. 67, 68
Wright, Dionisius 16, 17, 19
  Edward 62
  John 19, 45, 46, 53, 69
  Tho 44
Wrugy, Wm. 39
Wyat(t), Francis 3, 8, 43
Wyth(e), Fran 39
  G. 36
  George 31

Yardley/Yeardley, George 27, 30
Yeales, Tho. 38
Yewren, And. 60
Young, ___ 44,
  Mr. 75
  Alexander 67
  Henry 50
  John 20, 65
  Tho. 39, 56, 73

www.ingramcontent.com/pod-product-compliance
Lightning Source LLC
Chambersburg PA
CBHW031426290426
44110CB00011B/550